P9-BYE-428

www.brookscole.com

www.brookscole.com is the World Wide Web site for Brooks/Cole and is your direct source to dozens of online resources.

At *www.brookscole.com* you can find out about supplements, demonstration software, and student resources. You can also send email to many of our authors and preview new publications and exciting new technologies.

www.brookscole.com
Changing the way the world learns®

WRITING
WITH STYLE

APA Style for Social Work

Second Edition

Lenore T. Szuchman
Barry University

Barbara Thomlison
Florida International University

THOMSON

BROOKS/COLE   Australia • Canada • Mexico • Singapore • Spain • United Kingdom • United States

THOMSON

BROOKS/COLE

Executive Editor: *Lisa Gebo*
Assistant Editor: *Alma Dea Michelena*
Editorial Assistant: *Sheila Walsh*
Marketing Manager: *Caroline Concilla*
Marketing Assistant: *Mary Ho*
Signing Representative: *Miguel Ortiz*
Project Manager, Editorial Production:
Katy German

Print/Media Buyer: *Doreen Suruki*
Permissions Editor: *Elizabeth Zuber*
Production Service: *Shepherd, Inc.*
Copy Editor: *Patterson Lamb*
Cover Designer: *Rokusek Design*
Printer: *Thomson West*

COPYRIGHT © 2004 Brooks/Cole, a division of Thomson Learning, Inc. Thomson Learning™ is a trademark used herein under license.

ALL RIGHTS RESERVED. No part of this work covered by the copyright hereon may be reproduced or used in any form or by any means— graphic, electronic, or mechanical, including but not limited to photocopying, recording, taping, Web distribution, information networks, or information storage and retrieval systems— without the written permission of the publisher.

4 5 6 7 07 06

For more information about our products, contact us at:
Thomson Learning Academic Resource Center
1-800-423-0563

For permission to use material from this text, contact us by: **Phone: 1-800-730-2214**
Fax: 1-800-730-2215
Web: http://www.thomsonrights.com

ISBN 0-534-62182-1

Brooks/Cole—Thomson Learning
10 Davis Drive
Belmont, CA 94002
USA

Asia
Thomson Learning
5 Shenton Way #01-01
UIC Building
Singapore 068808

Australia/New Zealand
Thomson Learning
102 Dodds Street
Southbank, Victoria 3006
Australia

Canada
Nelson
1120 Birchmount Road
Toronto, Ontario M1K 5G4
Canada

Europe/Middle East/Africa
Thomson Learning
High Holborn House
50/51 Bedford Row
London WC1R 4LR
United Kingdom

Latin America
Thomson Learning
Seneca, 53
Colonia Polanco
11560 Mexico D.F.
Mexico

Spain/Portugal
Paraninfo
Calle/Magallanes, 25
28015 Madrid, Spain

Contents

CHAPTER 14

Preparing a Poster Presentation **155**

APPENDIXES

Preface

You may believe that good writing comes naturally for some people, but even for the experienced writer it is hard work. Educators of social workers have long recognized the importance of writing, yet little time in social work education is devoted to improving writing skills. Increasingly, the context in which social work graduates practice demands that social workers be proficient not just in assessment and intervention skills but also in writing skills. In fact, the development of high-quality writing skills is not only desirable but may even be critical when legal and managed care issues arise. At all levels of social work education and professional practice, writing skills are intrinsic to competency skills. Writing plays a vital role in all courses and most social work practice settings; early and sustained attention to improving writing skills is essential to developing confidence and maintaining it in professional practice.

In response to this issue, we developed *Writing With Style*. This book is created for students and professionals who use the style of the American Psychological Association (APA) for writing scholarly papers. It has a single purpose—to promote improvement in the writing of scholarly papers in the style described in the Fifth Edition of the *Publication Manual of the American Psychological Association*. *Writing With Style* will assist students, professionals, and academics in thinking about and understanding how to write in the style used in scholarly journals. Using the practice examples you develop in this book, you will learn to write the basic elements of scholarly papers, a skill essential to education and practice in social work.

Writing With Style: APA Style for Social Work can be used in several courses. It is an excellent companion for social work research and practice methods courses. It can also be used in introductory graduate courses and in integrative research and field education seminars, evaluation research, and any elective courses with writing requirements. Many social work course assignments call for students to provide review articles, methodological papers, research proposals, poster presentations, and other writings. From this book, students can learn the proper APA format for those projects, including details such as writing titles, preparing tables, organizing references, and avoiding common writing errors. The exercises throughout the book encourage active learning and reinforce the basic elements of writing with APA style that supplements any course work. Using this book may even assist students and professionals in less formal aspects of written work such as documenting their practice, keeping journals, and writing case studies. With this book as a reference source for assignments and papers, social work students will be less intimidated by having to write papers using APA style. Practicing social workers can use this book to refresh these writing skills and learn about style standards that may have been revised since they graduated. Social work academics can use this book as a handy reference guide for manuscript preparation and grading of student assignments. The book's informal, easy-to-read style makes it suitable for a wide audience who need a quick reference to the basic and essential elements of writing with style using the APA guidelines.

The goals of this book are (a) to reduce confusion about writing in APA style, (b) to improve technical and scholarly writing skills in social work education and practice, and (c) to demonstrate the value and importance of developing writing skills. Most social work students, whether undergraduate or graduate level, need to improve their writing skills, both for educational performance and for professional practice. Once students master the basic elements of APA style, they will have the motivation and confidence to continue improving their writing.

As a primer in the elements of APA style, this book should be used early in the student's social work education. However, students and professionals at any point in their social work education can benefit from the practical tips and guidelines contained in the book. We think *Writing With Style* will address writing issues in many settings—the classroom, the field, and conference presentations. We hope that it will make reading more enjoyable and using APA style guidelines less overwhelming and more understandable.

Making Sense of APA Style Format

APA style writing is a skill requiring a substantial amount of practice. Social work students are usually expected to conform to APA guidelines in all their written work, including that assigned in research methods classes. Sometimes the transition from first-year English composition classes to social work classes leaves students confused because these first-year classes tend to be taught with emphasis on the Modern Language Association (MLA) style. In these courses students generally learn how to organize a coherent paragraph, how to develop a thesis statement, and how to write an essay or a library research paper in the generic (MLA-based) style. This is a useful start, but it does not enhance students' technical writing skills when it comes to using APA guidelines.

Shortly after admission to the social work program, students must master a technical writing style that often contradicts what they learned in their first-year composition classes. They must now learn to write using APA style, which includes not only rules made explicit in the *Publication Manual* but also other conventions that constitute the unwritten rules of APA style. For example, rather than write about what other authors *said* or *believed,* they should concentrate on what the authors *found* or *reported.* Also, the title of an article should not be mentioned in a literature review, and passive voice may sometimes be used.

Learning by Doing

In this book, you will learn about scholarly writing through modeling the writing of published authors. Completing the exercises in this book will familiarize you with APA style by a method that also helps you begin to read APA publications. The exercises require you to scan APA publications for examples of particular rules and conventions. You then learn by modeling or practicing these techniques. You can use the lists you generate by completing the exercises in *Writing With Style* when you write your own papers—the words and phrases contained in the exercises exemplify not only APA style but also the social work scholar's tone and form. Thus, you benefit both from the *process of searching* for examples in social work journals and from the *item file* you develop for use in writing your review articles, methods papers, and other written work.

It is daunting for the undergraduate social work student to see the *Publication Manual* and realize that all writing must conform to a style set out in what looks like a reference book rather than a style guide. In fact, the *Publication Manual* is both. And many students, even many professionals, need help in using it. For example, there are some rules in the *Publication Manual* that writers *must* learn, and there are others that they do not have to learn until these rules are relevant or needed for writing. That is, some rules must become second nature (e.g., the use of past tense for the research method of a study), and others are used only occasionally and do not have to be memorized (e.g., how to reference a court case). The exercises in this book focus on the rules that should be learned while pointing to the types of things that should be looked up.

Throughout this book, we call attention to the need for precision in word usage. Students new to scholarly writing have not always been trained to seek the type of precision required. For example, we point out that when directing readers to consult a figure or a table, it is important to think about which verbs are possible if *table* is the subject of a sentence. Likewise, writers should consider which verbs are possible when a research design is the subject; research designs cannot *try* to do anything, for example.

Using the Book

We have attempted to make this book user friendly with an emphasis on technical writing in an easy-to-understand presentation. After chapter 1, which introduces you to why social work scholarship requires APA style, the *order of the chapters is flexible*. Chapter 2 discusses the ethics of writing, indicating the acceptable forms and practices of recognizing the ideas and intellectual property of others. Many writers understand scholarly misconduct or plagiarism, but many do not. And because this book is about learning and improving your written work, we strongly suggest that all readers consult this section before preparing any written assignments. Some will be surprised to learn that certain of their writing habits may qualify as scholarly misconduct or plagiarism and are unacceptable scholarly practices. After readers complete a few of the exercises, the concept of plagiarism should be clearer than before.

Chapter 3 contains general conventions, such as how to refer to the work of others in the body of a paper and tips for avoiding sexist language. It is general enough to be applicable to any section of a written paper or research report. Writing the specific sections of a paper is covered in chapters 4 through 11 in the order that many instructors teach them. But remember, they may be assigned in another order with no confusion for students. Chapter 12 contains guidance on avoiding the grammar and punctuation errors commonly found in social work papers. These include how to identify and avoid run-on sentences, how to use a colon, and how to apply rules accurately. These reflect the pet peeves of many professors. Students are encouraged to add notes on rules whose violations constitute the pet peeves of their own instructors.

Chapter 13 contains advice on rewriting. Beginning writers often assume that proofreading and revising are the same. We clarify the difference, then make several specific suggestions for revising. Next, we lead readers through a series of proofreading exercises that direct them to rely on their word processors to spot areas of potential problems. We encourage you to turn to these chapters early in the writing process. If you are using this book for a course, for example, chapters 12 and 13 can be consulted at any point in the development of an assigned paper.

The chapter on poster presentations, chapter 14, is last because it provides readers with a real-world option for communicating scholarly thinking and findings. In fact, we think all students benefit from the experience of developing a poster presentation in preparation for participating in case presentations, practice, and research conferences. Poster presentations teach social workers to integrate content and highlight key elements of a social work topic or research study, and for these reasons it is important for students to practice this skill before graduation. We think that professionals using this book will find this chapter very helpful because they may often be preparing poster presentations for conferences without having had any training for it in their degree programs. The appendixes contain outline samples of writing in APA style, including a proposal and research report, a theoretical review paper, a title page, and an abstract for a manuscript. We hope these samples are helpful, and we encourage you to model your work after them.

Social workers should not expect this book to replace the *Publication Manual*. They should be aware that this is one of several reference books that belong on their desk when they write. The exercises in *Writing With Style* do not cover every writing situation described in the *Publication Manual*. Instead, we provide general descriptions for writing social work research papers by condensing material from the *Publication Manual* and by including the most relevant information for review papers and research proposals, and we give primary emphasis to areas that social work students often find most difficult. Because almost everyone needs additional practice with certain basic grammar and punctuation rules, we also provide general rules throughout *Writing With Style*. We hope that you improve your writing and scholarly skills as a result of your use of this book.

New in the Second Edition

Most important, we have made the book current with the fifth Edition of the *Publication Manual* (2001). We have tried to keep this volume brief so that it can be used as a supplement for a variety of courses. However, lots of people and books gain weight over the years. In response to suggestions from readers and reviewers, we have included a few items in this volume that will make it possible for students to rely less on the *Publication Manual*. These additions include, for example, more details about creating tables and more examples of referencing. There are numerous smaller additions as well, such as details on hyphenation and formats for typing headers on manuscripts. We have expanded coverage on Internet issues, including referencing, plagiarizing, and a bit about selecting appropriate professional sites.

Acknowledgments

Again, we would like to acknowledge the many people whose observations, suggestions, and advice assisted us in the preparation of the first edition. A special thanks is due to Dr. Bruce A. Thyer, School of Social Work, University of Georgia, who is an inspiration in scholarly publications and who provided many worthwhile suggestions for improving the draft manuscript. Thanks also to Dr. Michael Rothery, Faculty of Social Work, the University of Calgary, who contributed eloquent comments and supportive suggestions to this project. We wish to thank Mayling Chu, California State University, Stanislaus; Dennette Derzotes, University of Illinois at Urbana–Champaign; Christopher Chacha, Alabama A&M; Michael Rothery, University of Calgary; Suzanne Weaver, Cedar Crest College; and Miriam Clubok, Ohio University; for carefully reviewing and providing many helpful suggestions for improving the second edition of the book.

A special thanks is due to the many students and colleagues who have taken the time to communicate to us just how helpful the book was in their social work and education courses.

We are indebted always to Lisa Gebo, Executive Editor, at Brooks/Cole Wadsworth Publishing for her effervescent encouragement and support. Also we appreciate the suggestions of Alma Dea Michelena, Assistant Editor, and her attention to this revised edition.

Finally, we would like to thank our own families, who remain supportive and encouraging.

Lenore T. Szuchman *LSzuchman@mail.barry.edu*
Barbara Thomlison *Barbara.Thomlison@fiu.edu*

1
Writing With Style

This is not a typical book about writing. It is an active learning guide designed to help beginning students and scholars of social work develop and practice the skills needed to write using APA style and format. Acquiring knowledge about the helping process and working with people and their environments both involve not only communicating verbally but also communicating in writing. Learning to practice as a professional requires writing as a professional social worker, which is easier said than done. This book is designed to help you write with the appropriate style, thereby improving your written assignments on your pathway to becoming a professional social worker.

The Stylistic Distinction

The scholarly articles in social work journals are different in style and presentation from the popular psychology books on human behavior found on the shelves of your local bookstore. The best of those books translate the findings of research on human behavior into language that makes the information easy for the nonscientific reader to access and apply. By contrast, you are expected to write your papers in an entirely different fashion. Now that you are enrolled in a social work program, you have, to some extent, already moved beyond the point of reading the self-help and popular psychology books (although these books will continue to provide enjoyment for you). You will be reading the scholarly journals read by professional social workers and preparing written assignments for your professor. Your instructor will expect your writing to reflect the scientific approach and scholarly quality of the journal articles you are reading.

Professionals read different scholarly materials with attention to different levels of detail. Not all professionals read with the same focus. The reader who is highly expert in a certain area of research or practice might be most interested in the Design, Method or Implications section of an article. The person who skims needs to be able to predict where the hypotheses will be and where the most important outcome will be. Finally, a student or researcher studying an area needs to check the reference list to see what further reading might be warranted.

You can see that if all parts of an article are written in a standardized way, each reader's needs can be met efficiently. For the sake of clarity, this kind of writing can get repetitive, but it can still be interesting to read—and in the best examples, the prose is fluid and elegant. Certainly, one hopes that the research findings alone generate excitement in at least a few readers. However, there can be no suspense, no teasing about the problems or their solutions, no surprise endings. If generating suspense were important, the first thing to do would be to eliminate the abstract. Even topic sentences for paragraphs detract from suspense. And if thrills were important, we would first list results that support the hypotheses, instead of listing them in the order in which the hypotheses were originally presented. Surprise endings? Not for professionals. They decide whether to read a research article or report only after knowing how the study came out.

Okay, you are ready to agree that professionals need a prose style different from that needed by the general public. But why do different professionals need different rules? Why can't everyone use Modern Language Association (MLA) or *The Chicago Manual of Style* rules? One reason is that different professions rely on different methods and different styles of argument. Social workers and psychologists need a format different from that of historians or literary critics. They have their own type of information to convey and their own values as consumers of their own literature. The National Association of Social Workers (NASW) and other social work organizations publish information within the social work community through an increasing number of scholarly journals. The numerous journals devoted to social work, social welfare, social work research, social work research in practice, and the social work community reflect a trend to publishing specializations in social work education, practice, and research (Mendelsohn, 1997; Thyer, 1994). The editors of these journals consider thousands of submissions each year. The rules set forth in the *Publication Manual of the American Psychological Association,* fifth edition (2001), facilitate the handling of such a large number of manuscripts by standardizing much of the format. These rules have been so convenient for readers and writers that many other science and social science journals adhere to a similar framework.

You will certainly want to own the *Publication Manual* and use it as a reference. But a reference book is just that—something you refer to when you are not sure of a rule. You are not expected to learn all the rules. No social worker submits a manuscript without having to look up some rules in the *Publication Manual* along the way. Why memorize the citation format for reviews of videos? For a non-English chapter in an edited book? Look it up—we all do.

Some conventions, however, need to be learned because you use them so often. Some are style rules you have encountered elsewhere, such as rules about agreement of subject and verb and when to use *between* versus *among,* and it's time you master these rules. Other conventions are unique to the social sciences, for example, using past tense for the results and present tense for the conclusions, abbreviating more liberally in the abstract than in the body of the paper, and using metric units whenever possible.

Unfortunately, there is more to sounding like a social worker than following all the style rules—just as there is more to sounding like a Texan than speaking English. If you want to sound like a Texan, you have to listen to a lot of Texans talk. If you want to write like a social worker, you have to read a lot of literature in social work and related disciplines. But even though it seems illogical, you must begin to learn how to write like a social worker even before you have the opportunity to read a lot of professional literature in social work.

Getting Started

This book is a reference for writing in APA style. It is both a rule book and a workbook. It is designed to prepare you to write your first social work paper or research report or to help you improve your writing after receiving disappointing grades for previous assignments. It will guide you through the social work literature in a way that will focus your attention on how authors use words and phrases. It will teach you to keep lists of examples of these words and phrases so that when you write papers, you can refer to your lists for models to help you construct sentences and paragraphs of your own. This book does *not* replace the *Publication Manual*. When you write papers, you should keep both the *Publication Manual* and this filled-in workbook near you. The *Publication Manual is* your *reference* book; this book is your *sample* book. If you want to produce a sentence or phrase like a more experienced writer of social work papers would, use your lists developed from these exercises. If you want to find out exactly how to organize, abbreviate, or punctuate a technical section, sentence, or phrase, use the *Publication Manual*. By the way, when you use the *Publication Manual* you may worry that it sometimes seems to contradict the printed format of the journals themselves. That is because your papers are *manuscripts,* and manuscripts differ from printed material. Your responsibilities are those of the author of a manuscript, not those of a printer preparing pages for a journal.

You will find two types of exercises in this book. The first and most frequently presented will result in the lists of usable sentences and phrases described above. To produce these lists, use sentence frames; that is, leave blanks for the words that are specific to the research being presented. For example, suppose you find the following sentence in a journal and it is an example of what you are looking for: "These findings regarding writing social work outcomes have several implications." Substitute a blank space when you copy it for your list of examples: "These findings regarding _____ have several implications." In most cases, we have sampled several journals and filled in the first few items for you with frames from our own search. Sometimes we have filled in the blanks for fun. Feel free to do the same with your own examples.

The second type of exercise is designed to help you understand a point of grammar by finding examples of it. These exercises are found in chapter 12, "Grammar and Punctuation Matters." Doing the exercises should help you learn the rules so that you never have to look them up again.

If you are using this book in a class, your instructor will guide you to the journals you should be looking at to do the various exercises. Otherwise, social work journals using APA format are suitable. However, you should be aware that whereas many journals are oriented to a specialized social work content or theoretical focus (such as *Social Work, Social Service Review,* and *Affilia: The Journal of Women and Social Work*), others accept an eclectic range of articles (e.g., *Journal of Family Issues*). Some publish the results of scholarly enquiry, notably, *Research on Social Work Practice* and *Social Work Research,* and still other journals specialize in review articles (e.g., *Journal of Clinical Psychology Review*). Unless otherwise noted, the assignments in this book require that you look at empirical research articles. You can find out whether APA guidelines are followed by a journal in a section called "Instructions to Authors" printed in any current edition of that journal.

If you are not being directed to specific journals to use, our advice is to sample from a variety of sources. Go to a computerized data base or to the library's current periodicals area and find a single issue of any of the following journals:

Child Abuse & Neglect: The International Journal

Child Welfare

Research on Social Work Practice

Social Service Review

Social Work Research

Social Work

An Exception

In preparing this book we have had to consider our own role as a model for writing. The journal articles you will read are designed to inform, not to amuse. They do not contain informal language, slang, contractions, or humor, and they do not address the reader as "you." If we were to write this book in that formal tone, it would be a good example for you, but it would not serve our purpose. Undoubtedly, you write in different ways for different purposes already. Now that you are learning the basic rules of a scientific style for a new purpose, we do not want you modeling your scientific prose on novels, newspapers, or textbooks—or any sources other than those specifically written in APA style. But textbooks do not necessarily benefit from such a style. Therefore, we have chosen not to conform strictly to APA tone in this book. However, we hope that you will not catch us making spelling, grammar, or punctuation errors. Please write to us (in care of Brooks/Cole) if you do!

2
Ethics and Writing

Aside from their presumed desire to lead lives that are honest, moral, and legal, scholars are also ethical in their writing because they enjoy the feeling of pride in a well-written paper that follows hard work and independent research. Reviewing the ethics of writing before starting to write is essential. Students are often surprised to learn of the variety of behaviors that contribute to integrity in scholarly writing. As professors we have learned that many students are still uncertain about what constitutes ethical writing even after several years in secondary school and college.

Your profession places high value on ethical conduct in practice with clients and this also includes ethical conduct in learning and writing about social work practice. When you submit your written assignment with your name on it, you are claiming everything in that work as yours unless you stipulate otherwise (Rothery, 2003). An excellent web site for a review of academic ethics in writing is The "Rules and Regs" Page: Thoughts and information on ethics in the academy *(http://fsw.ucalgary.ca/rothery)*. We have adapted with permission some of the content from this Web site for social work students.

One of the most common and important categories of misconduct in scholarly writing is *plagiarism*. Simply stated, plagiarism is taking or passing off ideas and writings from others as one's own. This includes using information and ideas from any published or unpublished source including books, chapters, articles, and manuals as well as information from the Internet. Plagiarism can be thought of as literary theft and is concerned with more than just using someone else's words. "Sometimes this is done unintentionally because of poor work habits, sometimes it is deliberate. In either case it is plagiarism and unacceptable" (Stefani & Carroll, 2001, p. 4).

Plagiarism is a form of cheating and "it is wrong (i.e. fraudulent), and therefore violates your internalized code of personal, academic and professional ethics. It also violates external codes of ethics and that can have various consequences, none of them pleasant." (http://fsw.ucalgary.ca/rothery/cheating.htm) It is not known exactly how much of the plagiarism found among students is unintentional. But whether the behavior is intentional or unintentional, the penalties may be severe and are certainly unpleasant. The cost in terms of time and emotional strain can be enormous. Preventive measures need to be taken. It is a writer's responsibility to cite a source correctly both when a work is quoted directly and when it is reconfigured. Reconfiguring an author's work may entail paraphrasing, summarizing, and modifying content and ideas. And finally, checking with the instructor is the best strategy for a student who remains confused and unclear about what constitutes plagiarism.

Thus, with plagiarism as with criminal law, ignorance is no excuse. By working through this book, you have committed yourself to the effort of sharpening your writing skills. Therefore, it is also a good time to consider the variety of misdeeds that you might accidentally commit when preparing your written scholarly work so that you can avoid them.

Using Exact Words and Sentence Structure

Everyone seems to know that using someone else's words without giving that author credit is unacceptable. This rule is quite simple to follow: Use quotation marks (or a block quote form) when you are using someone's exact words and indicate specifically where the original is to be found, including the page number. Failing to do this is plagiarism even if you attribute the ideas to the proper person, because in that case you have made it seem as if the ideas may have been borrowed but the words are your own.

Rothery (2003) cites White (1995) as an example, and has mentioned the author and date (White, 1995) just a few lines earlier. The following shows how this quotation appears in Rothery's website:

> "Suppose you are writing a paper on narrative theory applied
> to social work practice, and you are struck by the profundity
> and incisiveness of the following:

---

*Note: From Rothery (2003) The rules and regs page.
http://fsw.vcalgary.ca/rothery Adapted with permission.

There is always an unequal distribution of power in the therapeutic context, regardless of the steps that are taken by therapists to render the content of therapy more egalitarian. And as previously discussed, the potential for this unequal distribution of power to be disqualifying and objectifying of people is greater in team contexts. In view of this, it is important that steps be taken to counter possible toxic effects of this power imbalance, to reduce the potential for harm. One contribution to such steps is for reflecting team members to assist each other to deconstruct their responses. This can be achieved if team members invite each other to embody their comments with, or situate their speech acts in, the history of their personal experience, interests, intentions, imagination, and so on. If reflecting team members take responsibility to deconstruct their comments and questions in this way, this does provide at least some safeguard against the sort of imposition of "truth" that is the outcome of disembodied speech acts. (White, 1995, pp. 187–188)

If you take any part of this passage and place it verbatim in work of which you are the declared author, that is plagiarism. Michael White does not own the individual words he has used to compose this paragraph, but the patterning and purpose of the words are his intellectual property. If you use so much as a brief phrase from his work in yours, make sure it is clear that you are quoting, and give him credit."

Changing Words and Sentence Structure

Using the ideas of another author but not the words requires a reference to the source. For example, you want to present the information in the quote below in your work, but you feel it would fit better if written differently.

Of course, the relationship between clinical social workers and their clients is never truly equal, no matter how one tries to achieve this—and the imbalance is especially pronounced when a team of workers is part of the therapeutic effort (White, cited in Rothery, 1999).

Often, students would like to paraphrase ideas and give credit for them, but they cannot think of original ways to say them. Paraphrasing is a skill that takes some effort to acquire, so it is not surprising that when students find a useful thought in someone else's writing they are stymied about how a paraphrase can ever be better than the original. Some turn to the thesaurus to solve the problem. They leave the sentence more or less the way the author wrote it, but use a thesaurus to find words that might replace some of the original words. These students assume that once they change some words in another's work, the sentence no longer requires quotation marks and can legitimately be claimed as their own. If the following sentence is presented with no citation, it will still qualify as plagiarism even though some changes have been made:

> Regardless of the steps that are taken by therapists to be egalitarian, there is always an unequal distribution of power in the consulting room.

The writer is representing what is still White's work (cross-check it against the first sentence in the main quote) as her or his own, and a reader who assumes this sentence originated with someone other than White will be deceived.

Suppose you are a clear thinker and decide you should rewrite Michael White's work in plain English. This is always a challenge with postmodernist writers, but it is early in the term and you have not lost your energy and ambition yet. After considerable effort, you render White's passage as follows:

> It is seldom, if ever, possible for the social worker and client to have a truly equal relationship, especially when teams are used and the client has several workers to contend with. This can be damaging to clients if they feel that they have too little power or are being treated like a "case" rather than a real person. One way of guarding against this is for team members to encourage each other to share their own experiences and interests as they affect their response to the client's situation. To the extent that team members can make their reactions personal in this way, clients are less likely to feel dehumanized and disrespected.

This may have undergone enough reworking that shared credit for the outcome is appropriate, but it is still best to indicate that White got the writer started on the paragraph (despite the fact that it is considerably improved). There are different ways of accomplishing this:

> To paraphrase White (1995), it is seldom, if ever, possible for . . .

As White (1995) and others have pointed out in their discussions of the helping relationship, it is seldom, if ever, possible . . .

. . . To the extent that team members can make their reactions personal in this way, clients are less likely to feel dehumanized and disrespected (cf. *White, 1995*).

There is a way to be fairly safe from unintentional plagiarism. Never try to paraphrase one sentence at a time. Instead, first read through the whole section you wish to paraphrase, then write your paraphrase, but without looking at the original. Then, be sure to credit the *ideas* conveyed in the paraphrased sections to their author. If you must quote a phrase or a sentence, do so, using quotation marks for the quoted materials. But don't try to change the original just a bit and think it is a paraphrase.

Changing the Format

Now that you have learned to avoid violating someone's sentence structure, what about the structure of a larger unit? Suppose you find a literature review on the same subject as your own? What is the plagiarism risk in this case? If you organize the material around the same themes, you have plagiarized. If you use the same examples to make the same point, you have plagiarized. To prevent these forms of plagiarism, consider using the reference list of the literature review to help you with your own library work, but don't read the actual review article until you have drawn some conclusions of your own. Then when you find that the review author has made a point you would like to add to your own review, you can cite that author for having had a certain insight about some research that you have also read— but from which you did not gain the same insight. You can even cite the author of the literature review for finding themes in the literature that organized the topic in a useful way.

Borrowing and Recycling Ideas

What about borrowing ideas from your professor or your textbook? To be safe, you must give credit in those cases as well. You may well be expected to get your knowledge from these sources, but if you use that knowledge in a written product of your own, cite the sources. It is also unethical to use your own words for more than one class as if you had written them fresh for each class.

> If you prepared an assignment for one class and resubmit it for another, this is *deceptive*. Even if you do more work on it in the form of additions and revisions, it is deceptive to submit it as if it was prepared primarily for the assignment in question. There are grey areas—the work you do for one [written assignment] can legitimately build on work you have done for another. In these cases, it is your responsibility to check with the instructor, clarifying your plans and obtaining agreement with them (Rothery, 2003).

Each professor expects that work written to fulfill the requirements of a certain class will be submitted *only* for that class. After all, researchers are not permitted to publish the same paper in two journals. And no one is allowed to sell a product as new if it has already been used. If you have a paper already written that seems to serve the needs of another assignment, check with the second professor for guidance about how much of the paper needs to be refreshed before you recycle it for the second class.

Students sometimes have difficulty deciding when a statement needs a reference and when a point of view is their own. You do *not* need to cite someone else for your own opinions or for generally agreed-on facts or principles. Your own opinion is easy to identify. For example, you may say:

> Our practice experiences differ from the research findings of the Greenspan (1998) study. In many cases, children as well as other family members often desire ongoing contact with parents, siblings, and other relatives even though a permanent return home is not possible. Consequently, we suggest caution is needed in adopting the findings from the Greenspan study if working with seriously emotionally disturbed children.

By contrast, at least in social work, it is difficult to decide which facts are generally agreed-on. It is tempting to assume that everyone sees behavior exactly as you do. For example, most observers may agree that adolescence is a time when self-esteem is fragile. But wait: Are you as sure about that as you are about the fact that in the United

States adolescents are expected to attend school? In fact, when you talk about psychological constructs like self-esteem, you are very near the divide between fact and nonfact. If you cannot find a reference for your assertion about self-esteem, at least qualify it somewhat. Perhaps you can assert that there *seems* to be an emphasis in our culture on the fragility of adolescent self-esteem. If you have searched the literature on self-esteem, then you will have references at your disposal to cite when you make an assertion. Cite them and you are safe.

Technical Phrases and Attribution

Students new to a field may also be confused about when a phrase is a standard technical term and when it is an original term. You are free to use technical phrases without attribution. Usually it is safe to use effects that authors study (e.g., transfer of training) or variables they use (e.g., attitudes toward help-seeking) without quotation marks. If you use a short phrase that you are not sure should be attributed to an author, use no quotation marks, but do include a page reference along with the rest of the citation information.

You may have begun to wonder how you can be safe from committing plagiarism if you are copying sentences from published sources into this book for later use in your own papers. The reason you can do that is the same reason you can use a dictionary or a book of foreign phrases without fear of plagiarism. You need to learn how words are used before you can use them on your own. People who share a subculture, as do scholars in any discipline, tend to use words and even whole phrases in a particular way. As you do the exercises in this book, you will find that the same phrases keep appearing in the articles you scan. You may even have difficulty finding enough different examples of a given type to fill the spaces provided. As rich as the English language is, only a finite number of ways exist for phrasing a prediction or the results of a *t* test. When a form is used repeatedly, you are allowed to use it without fear that someone else "owns" it.

The Internet

The Internet has made plagiarism much easier. You can cut and paste whole sections of someone else's work into your own (not that you would!) without even transcribing it. This is, in fact, a big problem on college campuses, and several Web sites exist just to help instructors sift through student papers and find plagiarism from the Web and papers acquired through Web-based "paper mills." One problem even for honest folks is that many Web sites do not have authors or dates of publication. That seems to make it both difficult to cite (but check chapter 10 of this book to see how easy it is) and tempting to believe that the material is not "owned" so that using it is not stealing. Well, it is owned—even if the identity of the writer is not obvious. Try not to cut and paste from these sources. Print the whole Web site if your custom is to photocopy articles for your papers. Take notes from the screen if your habit is to do that in the library (rather than photocopying). A good guideline is to "use a little and give credit" (Talub, 2000, p. 7). In fact, that is just about the same advice we could give for print sources as well. Once you have used a little from a lot of sources, you have transformed the material into something of your own, and you have broken no laws.

3
General Writing Techniques

Even though social workers are concerned primarily with how they can help clients, it is striking that one of the most common topics they actually write about is each other. The fact is, a great part of scholarly writing about social work concerns the work previously done by other scholars in the discipline. The longest part of a published research study is often the introduction, in which the author surveys the research that led to the current study. Advanced students and researchers often write research proposals that emphasize the same type of material found in the introductions of printed articles. Finally, students are often assigned to write literature reviews as term papers. Therefore, it is very important to learn what the *Publication Manual* has to say about referring to and conveying the ideas and findings of other authors. Likewise, it is valuable to search some journals to see what generalizations can be made about unwritten rules.

Referring to Other Authors

When you refer to the work of another author or authors, use last names only and do not mention the titles of their works. Always name the author or authors of the chapter you have read in an edited book, not the editor of the book. The publication year is a necessary part of the citation, but it is seldom presented as part of the sentence. Students often write, "In 1995, Thomlison did a study of . . ." However, it is much more appropriate to keep the year in parentheses unless you are making a special point of the date. When referring to the same study twice within a single paragraph, include the year in only the first instance.

Refer to other authors by last name only and do not mention the titles of their work (except in the References section).

You have the option of inserting the author's name and year of publication in parentheses: "A study of children who received treatment foster care interventions revealed that they are more likely to return to less restrictive environments than children receiving group care interventions" (Thomlison, 1992). If you do this, however, you *cannot* also include the author in the body of the same sentence. An example of this type of *error* is the following sentence: "Thomlison's study of children in treatment foster care has revealed they are more likely to return to less restrictive environments than children receiving group care" (Thomlison, 1992).

Another problem with regard to citations is how to refer to works that you have not read. First, try to get every relevant article and read it. However, you may cite material from secondary sources when you have not read the originals. Be aware that this does not allow you to put the sources you have not read yourself (primary sources) on your reference list. Put the source you *read* in the References section. In the body of the paper, you can mention the original work and indicate that you found mention of it in a secondary source—which you *do* cite: "Corcoran (as cited in Szuchman & Thomlison, 1999) found evidence that planned and systematic efforts to produce change in clients resulted in increased positive outcomes compared to unplanned and inconsistent efforts." Szuchman and Thomlison will be on your reference list; Corcoran will not. See page 9 in chapter 2 of this book for an example. We cite Rothery who cites White. Now look in our references list at the end of this book and see which of these two authors is listed.

If you have not read a source, do not list it in your References section. In the body of the paper refer to the source you did read (secondary source) and indicate that the primary source was cited in the secondary source.

Refer to Exercise 1 at the end of the chapter

A potential source of confusion exists when referring to someone else's research as the "current" study, the "present" study, or "this" study. These terms always refer to the study reported in the Method and Results sections of the article you are reading (or the research report you are writing). When you are looking at an article and writing about the outcome of that author's study in your own paper, you may come across these phrases and they may find their way into your description of that study. Do not allow this. You may confuse your readers even more than this paragraph has confused you! And for the same reason.

Do not use "the current study" or "the present study" to refer to someone else's work.

One feature of our profession is that social workers are very polite when disagreeing with colleagues or disapproving of their work. You should be sensitive to this tone in your own reviews of the literature. A social worker who feels that Simpson has done a terrible study may only say "Other researchers have failed to replicate Simpson's result" or "Simpson may have failed to take into account the . . ." Be careful about your tone when describing a controversial issue. Present both sides and indicate what kind of data support one conclusion and what kind support the other.

Words and Phrases to Collect

The English language contains so many words and expressions that it may come as a surprise to know how often social workers stick to the same ones over and over again. This is actually of benefit to the new writer, because with a collection of stock words and phrases, anyone can *sound* like a social worker, even while still learning to *think* like one. In this section you will create a collection of some of these words and phrases to sprinkle into your own writing.

First, consider how often sentences in a literature review are constructed around a researcher or a research study as the grammatical subject, for example, "Fraser and Thyer (1991) demonstrated that . . ." You may be tempted to vary your sentences by choosing the author as the grammatical subject sometimes and the research study at other times. Be cautious about this. You are obligated to use verbs that logically suit the abilities of your grammatical subjects. People are capable of many activities (verbs), but studies can *do* hardly anything. Consider this problem whenever you are tempted to begin a sentence with "The study . . ." Exactly what can a study do?

Refer to Exercises 2, 3, and 4 at the end of the chapter

You may have noticed in completing the previous three exercises that authors often use passive voice verb constructions when discussing a study, an outcome, or a theory. For example, they will note that a study *was designed* for some purpose. That type of writing shows you that the author knows that studies themselves can't assess or find or test. Authors design studies so that they (the authors) can assess things.

In contrast to inanimate studies and abstractions such as theories, a researcher or group of researchers can very easily perform actions. Consequently, sentences focusing on researchers are fairly easy to formulate. In this case, look for sentences in which the subject of a sentence is a specific author or authors or a more general noun referring to a human, such as *author, researcher,* or *investigator.*

Refer to Exercise 5 at the end of the chapter

> Use a person (e.g., "the researcher" or a proper name) rather than a product (e.g., a study or a finding) as a sentence subject whenever possible.

Now that you know 20 things that social workers *do*, please take note of the words you did *not* find. You probably did not find *feel*. Research studies cannot feel, and researchers keep their feelings to themselves. Also, you found less thinking and believing than you might have expected. Perhaps *believe* doesn't convey the scientific attitude as well as *hypothesize* does. Likewise, researchers very often *reason,* but it seems as if they hardly ever *think*. Another group of words that will be rare in your lists is related to writing and talking: *stated, wrote, said.* Journalists and literary critics are interested in what people say and write. Social workers refer to the writings of others to report what they found or investigated.

> Do not indicate what researchers thought, felt, believed, or said.

Another type of verb that social workers use can be categorized as a "hedge word." We hedge even when we hold strong opinions about why people behave as they do, because usually we cannot be absolutely sure of cause and effect. Even the most carefully designed studies do not provide ironclad evidence that allows us to generalize with absolute certainty about behavior. Therefore, we avoid using confident language (e.g., the kind you just read in the previous sentence) when we are making claims about behavior. *May* and *might* are our primary hedge words: "Certain functions may decline with age; it may be fruitful to consider gender in the context of family settings." Sometimes we hedge outside of the verb phrase, for example, "One possible interpretation is . . ." Also, don't forget that hypothesis testing is another excuse for a hedge word. For example, results support a hypothesis, they seldom confirm it—and they never prove it.

Refer to Exercise 6 at the end of the chapter

Transition words and phrases help connect the discussion of one study to that of another. They also guide the reader through the logic of the sequence of paragraphs. They can make your writing more precise. Look for them at the beginning of sentences, set off by commas.

Refer to Exercise 7 at the end of the chapter

Words and Phrases to Avoid

The *Publication Manual* offers many examples of writing errors to avoid. This section merely highlights some common student bloopers. It would be wise for students also to look over the chapter entitled "Expressing Ideas and Reducing Bias in Language" in the *Publication Manual*.

Errors We Have Already Noted

1. The *current* or *present* study when referring to someone else's work in your literature review

2. Authors' first names

3. Titles of articles in your literature review

4. The word *prove* (substitute the word *support*)

5. The feelings and thoughts of the researchers you cite

6. What other authors *stated, said,* or *wrote*

Wordiness and Redundancy

Wordiness and redundancy are not the same. You should avoid using more words than you need (e.g., *based on the fact that = because*), and you should also try not to say the same thing twice (e.g., *could be perhaps because = could be because*). Your main concern, however, is to eliminate *all* unnecessary words. Don't bother doing this until you have completed the drafts related to organization and clarity. But by the time you are on your third or fourth draft (We realize that we're asking you to commit yourself to quite a few drafts!), look for words you can cross out without changing any meanings. Here are examples.

1. *The results revealed that* . . . Omit the entire phrase and start your sentence with the word that would come next.

2. *The obtained data showed* . . . Where else would data come from if it had not been obtained? Just say *The data showed.*

3. *Participants for the study were* . . . Of course they were for the study. Just say *Participants were.*

4. . . . *due to the fact that* . . . Just say *because.*

5. *The reason is because* . . . Just say *The reason is.*

6. *A total of eight participants* . . . Just say *Eight participants.*

7. *The results were statistically significant* . . . This is science you are reporting. Of course you are using *significant* in its statistical sense. Omit *statistical.*

8. . . . *has been previously found* . . . The verb is past tense, so it must have occurred previously. Omit *previously.*

9. *In her study, White (1997) found* . . . Of course that's where she found it. Omit *In her study.*

10. *Distinctly different* . . . Choose one.

Over-Reliance on Passive Voice

APA style is more relaxed about allowing passive voice constructions than some other styles. But sometimes writers get so tangled up in sentences they don't realize that changing to the active voice can be really easy. Here are some common examples:

1. *Participants were administered a questionnaire (drug, test, interview, and so on)*. Examiners can administer a test. Tests can be administered. But what do participants do? They *take* a test. They *fill in* or *complete* a questionnaire. Perhaps you can't resist the passive voice: They *were interviewed*. Fine.
2. *The study was designed by Rubin to . . .* Whenever you have the passive voice verb followed by the word *by*, you have all you need—you know who did it. This type of construction is so easy to switch to active that you might as well do so: *Rubin designed a study to . . .*

Informal Language and Slang

The tone of technical writing is not colloquial, that is, conversational or informal. The *Publication Manual* provides the example of *write up* as an informal, perhaps imprecise, way of saying *report*. Slang is the most informal type of language. Examples include *blooper* to mean *error* and *no-no* to mean *something that is forbidden*. (Notice that our use of these words is acceptable—we are not writing a research report.) Students usually know that slang is a *no-no*, and they avoid that type of *blooper*. Be on the lookout (that is, *search*) for informal language in your scholarly writing.

- Contractions are absolutely unacceptable. Use apostrophes only to indicate possession. Remember that when pronouns contain possessive meanings they do so without apostrophes (e.g., its, hers).

- Do not be afraid to use *because. Because* is a lovely, precise word. *Being that* is a poor replacement. *Since* is specifically made unacceptable for this purpose in the *Publication Manual. Since* is used to mean *after that time*.

- Use *while* (like *since*) in its temporal sense only. Hunt for *while* in your papers. If you can't substitute *simultaneously,* change it, perhaps to *although* or *whereas.*

- Do not be afraid to use *and.* Indulge yourself. *And* is often the best substitute for *while.* See how many wordy phrases you can eliminate by replacing them with *and.*

Long Quotes and Frequent Short Quotes

Because we strive for clarity and economy of expression, seldom is there need for a long quotation. Literary criticism, by contrast, would be nowhere without the long quote. The way someone else says something is vital to what literary critics have to say about it. But technical styles are seldom quotable. If you are reporting on someone else's research, just summarize the author's point. Perhaps the author has used a word in a new way; if so, place quotation marks around that word. The *Publication Manual* has a rule about how to cite page numbers when quoting from another's work and special rules about indenting long quotations (see Chapter 10 of this book).

It is easy to sympathize with someone who would like to avoid plagiarism and avoid short quotations at the same time. Sometimes you may feel that there is no efficient way to convey the contents of a certain phrase (e.g., "responses were scored for speed and accuracy") except in the author's words. One way to solve this problem is to take a stretch and get a drink of water when you feel a short quotation coming on. Then when you sit down to write again, write that sentence without looking at the source. If it still comes out very close to the original, you can put the page reference in at the end of the paraphrase.

Avoid long quotations and frequent brief quotations.

The Editorial We

Students are often taught (in classes other than social work classes) to avoid the use of *I* and that one alternative is to refer to yourself in the third person: the author. In social work papers, however, that is absolutely out of the question. The other option is to refer to yourself as *we.* This is called the "editorial we" (as distinguished from the "royal we," which kings and queens use to refer to themselves). It is common in some styles to use the "editorial we," but the *Publication Manual* expressly advises against it. You are perfectly within your rights to use *I* in a social work paper (and you are allowed to use *we* to refer to the authors if your paper has more than one author). Sometimes the passive voice is used instead but with less than optimum results: "It was hypothesized that . . ." Usually the best solution is to remember that it's not about you. Refocus the sentence on something other than yourself: "The hypothesis was . . ."

Do not refer to yourself as "we."

The Use of You

Do not affect a tone that implies an interaction with the reader. In a research report there is never a reason to address the reader of the work (as we do throughout this textbook).

Nor is it permitted to use the word *you* instead of *one* in speaking of a hypothetical person. For example, "When you reach middle age, your vision and hearing have already begun to decline." This should be written in the third person: "When one reaches middle age, vision and hearing have already begun to decline."

Do not call the reader "you."

The One-Sentence Paragraph

Every paragraph requires a topic sentence. Putting a topic sentence at the beginning of every paragraph will help you to achieve a crisp, clear, and well-organized style. Putting the topic sentence elsewhere in the paragraph (as you may have been encouraged to do in a previous writing class) detracts from the goal. If you find you have written a one-sentence paragraph, you must evaluate the organizational plan that allowed this to happen. Ask yourself, what is the topic of the paragraph? Is the sentence a topic sentence with no further elaboration of the topic? If so, perhaps you forgot to elaborate. Is your single sentence really a bit of elaboration belonging to a topic that already has its own paragraph? Then move it. Is it by itself because it is actually all you really know about that subject? Perhaps your paper would be improved if you omit things you know so little about.

Start every paragraph with a topic sentence and never write one-sentence paragraphs.

Unbiased Language

You probably know that it is no longer acceptable to use *he* when you are referring to a person who could be either male or female. The *Publication Manual* advises you not to use the unpronounceable combination forms *s/he* or *(s)he*. It is also unacceptable to switch between *he* and *she* as if either form could be used generically. You may use *he or she* and similar constructions, but sentences become unnecessarily cumbersome when you do: "The participant filled out his or her questionnaire using his or her code number." Of the various alternatives, try to find one that eliminates the need for the singular pronoun completely. Using *his or her* every time you find that you need a possessive is not as convenient as using *their*. However, be sure that you have used a plural noun prior to replacing *his or her* with *their*. It is a very common error to begin the sentence with a singular individual and then talk about *their* score. If you begin with one person, you must then refer to *his or her* score. The solution is to use the plural (people, participants, students, etc.) and then discuss *their scores*. You have thereby avoided both sexist language and an inappropriate pronoun. For the example above, the best solution would be "Participants filled out their questionnaires using their code numbers."

Do not write "he" when you mean "he or she."

Using Prefixes

A few prefixes are used quite often in social work papers. They include *non, pre, post,* and *sub*. Please remember that prefixes cannot stand alone with spaces on both sides. They must be attached to words. They may be attached with hyphens or just attached directly onto the root words. The *Publication Manual* will give you guidance if you are not sure in a given case. However, you can be very sure that if they stand alone, you have made a mistake. If you test nonsmokers and smokers in your study, be sure you write *nonsmokers* and not *non smokers*.

Do not leave prefixes hanging loose from words.

Incorrect Plurals

Many professors will be annoyed if you do not use the following plurals correctly: *data, criteria, phenomena, stimuli,* and *hypotheses.* The singular forms are *datum, criterion, phenomenon, stimulus,* and *hypothesis.* You will probably never need to use *datum,* but try to learn to use a plural verb with data.

These words are plural nouns: data, criteria, phenomena, stimuli, and hypotheses.

Mixed-up Latin Abbreviations

You probably find yourself writing *et al., i.e.,* and *e.g.* a lot now. But where do the periods and commas really go? The commas go after *i.e.* and *e.g. every* time you write them. What about the periods? The periods go after abbreviations. Here's what these three abbreviations mean:

- The abbreviation *et al.* means *et alia,* which means "and other things." If you remember that *et* is not an abbreviation but rather a Latin word meaning "and," you will remember that there is no reason to put a period after it. By contrast, *al.* is an abbreviation, so it requires a period.

- Next, *i.e.* stands for *id est,* the Latin phrase meaning "that is." Both letters in this Latin abbreviation are legitimate abbreviations, so they both take periods. When you need this phrase, use the Latin abbreviation (i.e.) inside parenthetical elements and the English phrase (that is) in all other instances. Both are followed by commas.

- Finally, *e.g.* stands for *exempli gratia,* the Latin phrase meaning "for example." As with i.e., these letters are both abbreviations, so both take periods. Also as with i.e., use the Latin abbreviation (e.g.) inside parentheses and the English equivalent (for example) in all other instances. Both are followed by a comma.

Learn how to punctuate et al., i.e., and e.g.

Use of Acronyms

An acronym is a "word" made up of the first letters of a group of words. There will be times when you will read or want to use an acronym. Some of you will already be familiar with, for example, the acronyms for the National Association of Social Workers (NASW), Master of Social Work (MSW), and the American Psychological Association (APA). Also, many social work and psychological measuring instruments are referred to by their acronyms, such as CBCL (Child Behavior Checklist) and FACES (Family Adaptability and Cohesion Scale). At first occurrence the name must be written out with the acronym in parentheses immediately following to indicate that from that point forward you will use the acronym when referring to that group of words. And then don't forget to use only the acronym afterward.

Exercise 1

Copy examples of secondary sources cited in the text of a literature review or similar article.

1. Hudson's Self-Esteem Scale (cited in Corcoran & Fischer, 1994) . . .

2. _____

_____

3. _____

_____

4. _____

_____

Exercise 2

Select several articles that cover topics of your interest or that have been assigned in your course. Find verbs in which the grammatical subject of a sentence is someone's *study, work, experiment,* and *research*. It may also be useful to include the object of that verb.

1. employs methods

2. demonstrates

3. provides evidence

4. _____

5. _____

6. _____

7. _____

8. _____

Exercise 3

Another nonhuman grammatical subject often found in research reports is the outcome of someone's research. The words to look for here are *findings, results, evidence*. Don't be surprised if the list you create for this exercise has a lot of overlap with the previous one.

List the verbs in sentences in which the subject is some kind of study *outcome*.

1. demonstrates

2. can be explained

3. suggests

4. _____

5. _____

6. _____

7. _____

8. _____

Exercise 4

What can theories do? What can be done to them?
Find the verbs that are used with *theories* or *hypotheses*.

1. take something as evidence

2. have been challenged

3. focus on

4. lead to the hypothesis that

5. _____

6. _____

7. _____

8. _____

 **Exercise 5**

List the verbs associated with _researchers_. (Here you have been given plenty of space for a long list.) When you find a verb used more than once, put a check mark next to it on this list every time you find it.

1. have shown

2. found

3. replicated

4. reported

5. _____

6. _____

7. _____

8. _____

9. _____

10. _____

11. _____

12. _____

13. _____

14. _____

15. _____

 **Exercise 6**

List some *hedges* from your articles.

1. suggests

2. appears to

3. is consistent with

4. _____

5. _____

6. _____

7. _____

8. _____

Exercise 7

List transition words and phrases.

1. Notably

2. In contrast

3. Similarly

4. _____

5. _____

6. _____

7. _____

8. _____

A common mistake is using a transition by itself (such as *on the other hand*) that requires the explicit use of a preceding one *(on the one hand)*. Also, if you are going to enumerate your points, use *first, second,* and *third*—not *firstly, secondly,* and *thirdly*. And don't use *second* if you haven't been explicit about *first*.

4
Writing an Introduction

The *APA Publication Manual* directs that the Introduction of a research proposal or research report should contain five components:

1. Scholarly review of relevant literature

2. Purpose of the study

3. Theoretical implications

4. Definitions of variables

5. Statement of hypotheses and their rationales

You will find that authors are often very explicit about these items. An article may even begin with the words "The purpose of the study was . . . " The final paragraphs of the Introduction may contain sentences that begin with "The specific hypotheses were . . . " And in between, you will find the literature review and theoretical implications of the current study.

The components of the introduction for a theoretical or review paper vary from a research focused paper. The introduction should contain the following four elements:

1. The topic, problem, question, or issue to be reviewed

2. Statement of the objectives of the review

3. Significance or relevance of the topic including the practical significance, theoretical significance, and social policy significance

4. Scope of the literature to be reviewed, including the inclusion or exclusion criteria of the literature for examination

5. Definition of key concepts or theoretical frameworks to be reviewed

6. Conclusion: A succinct statement of the topic/question being addressed

By the way, you are not allowed to use the word *Introduction* as a heading for this section. The *Publication Manual* instructs that you *not* label this section in your own paper. Its location indicates which section it is. In the publications themselves, however, sometimes the word *Introduction* does appear as a heading. Remember that the *Publication Manual is* directing authors of manuscripts, not printers of journals.

The Introduction section does not include the heading Introduction.

What Was Done and Why

The *Publication Manual* advises that the first paragraph or two of your paper should provide "a firm sense of what was done and why" (p. 11). In a review article you should indicate what the issue or problem is and why it is important to study or have more information about it.

Refer to Exercises 1 and 2 at the end of the chapter

Now consider how authors introduce their work. The first sentence of an article is always written with some strategy in mind. The author might want to demonstrate at the start the purpose or the importance of the issue. Or there might be other attention-grabbing ways to begin. However, beware of the temptation to overstate. No need to characterize the special problem you are studying as a national crisis. Your audience is most often made up of professional social workers. They do not expect the tone of their professional reading to be "ripped from the headlines."

Refer to Exercises 3 and 4 at the end of the chapter

Hypotheses need rationales: They are not supposed to be based on intuition or hunches. It is possible that early in the research process, a researcher did have a hunch. That hunch may even have led the researcher to begin the project, perhaps by beginning a literature search to find support for that hunch. By the time the literature has been reviewed, the author is supposed to be able to support the hypotheses with something more convincing than his or her original hunch. Researchers normally use previous results or theories to predict an outcome they expect a study to demonstrate. When writing your hypothesis, you are expected to explain why one group will score higher than another, for example, or why one type of intervention will be more effective than another in addressing a particular problem. This process is implicit in the entire literature review contained in the introduction. But it is good practice to make these reasons explicit at the point where the hypotheses are discussed.

Refer to Exercise 5 at the end of the chapter

Note that hypotheses often state a direction. That is, they make predictions that one group will perform better than another rather than just perform differently. In Example 3 in Exercise 5, the expectation might be specifically that alcohol-impaired drivers would not drive as well as the unimpaired group—not simply that one group (unspecified) would not drive as well as the other. When hypotheses do not contain a predicted direction of effect, they are sometimes called *research questions*. For example, a researcher might wish to compare two types of support group without a firm belief that one is better than the other. Sometimes these studies are called *descriptive*. In such case researchers want to learn *how* groups differ before they attempt to explain the reason or mechanism for the difference.

At times, neither research questions nor hypotheses are clearly stated in the study. This may happen when the research is at an exploratory level. In these instances, look for words such as *intent* or *purpose*.

Refer to Exercise 6 at the end of the chapter

Relevance of the Research Question

In trying to provide "a firm sense of what was done and why," writers sometimes have difficulty deciding how much methodological detail is appropriate in the introduction. Find statements referring to the method of the study being reported. Look for *the current study* or *the present study,* which authors use to distinguish their own study from others mentioned in the literature review. (Be careful *not* to use these words in your own literature review except to refer to the study you are either proposing or reporting.) Notice what issues of methodology the authors highlight in the introduction. They may try to distinguish the special nature of a control group, the elimination of a confound they have discovered in previous studies similar to their own, or some innovation they are contributing. These elements will be described in detail in the Method section, but may receive mention in the introduction because they clarify the rationale for the current study.

Refer to Exercise 7 at the end of the chapter

 **Exercise 1**

Select several articles from a variety of journals or use articles that have been assigned by your professor. Examining only the first two paragraphs of your research articles, copy the single sentence in each that states the purpose of the study. If you do not find such a sentence, try the last two paragraphs of the introduction.

1. Accordingly, the primary purpose of our study is to reexamine the family preservation findings of Fraser and Walton (1994), taking into consideration the quality and level of social support.

2. This research was conducted to determine variables that characterize perpetrators who show escalation in abusive behavior during times of stress.

3. Women are more likely to be diagnosed with depression than men. In the present study, we attempted to find a possible ecological explanation for this finding.

4. _____
_____
_____
_____

5. _____
_____
_____
_____

6. _____
_____
_____
_____

 **Exercise 2**

Still looking at only the first or last few paragraphs of the articles you have selected, find and copy sentences that indicate why this is an important research issue.

1. Knowledge of these factors may help identify individuals at risk for . . .

2. The problem under study here has implications for many social work theories as vitally important to the assessment of . . .

3. As knowledge of the consequences of child neglect has increased, investigators have become interested in . . .

4. _____

_____

_____

5. _____

_____

_____

6. _____

_____

_____

Exercise 3

Copy the first sentence from several articles. Indicate what type of information it contains. It is possible that some of the sentences you found for the previous two exercises held this place of honor in an article. For this exercise, however, do not recycle sentences from the previous exercises.

1. A shortage of foster homes over the past 20 years for the now 500,000 children in protective custody has jeopardized the quality of services provided to the nation's most vulnerable population. (This is stating a long-studied and serious problem, which is also why this study is important.)

2. Violence, juvenile delinquency, and criminal behavior, especially in urban-centered schools, are characteristic of some communities. (This is a statement of a well-known phenomenon.)

3. Violence is a learned behavior and thus amenable to prevention and change. (This is a definition.)

4. _____
   _____
   _____
   _____

5. _____
   _____
   _____
   _____

6. _____
   _____
   _____
   _____

Exercise 4

Now look at the final few paragraphs of the introduction. Find the specific hypotheses. Copy the sentences or phrases that tell you the hypotheses are being stated. Look for words such as *predict* or *expect* if you don't see what you are looking for right away.

1. Specific predictions were as follows . . .

2. It was anticipated that the ability to express empathy would affect the way in which social work practicum students assessed clients during the initial interview.

3. The use of a genogram and ecomap was expected to enhance parents' understanding of family strengths and weaknesses.

4. _____

_____

_____

_____

5. _____

_____

_____

_____

6. _____

_____

_____

_____

Exercise 5

Find examples of rationales for hypotheses. Some articles will not provide these in an explicit way just prior to or just after hypotheses have been stated. Do not use those articles for this exercise. Find examples of explicit rationales only.

1. If there are differences between flirting and sexual harassment in the workplace, differences between their effects on behavior could be expected.

2. From prior research with adult sexual-assault survivors, trauma related symptoms were expected to be evident in survivors of child sexual abuse.

3. Because our prior analysis pointed to the importance of avoiding alcohol when driving, . . .

4. _____
_____
_____
_____

5. _____
_____
_____
_____

6. _____
_____
_____
_____

Exercise 6

Find examples of the stated purpose or intent of a research study.

1. The purpose of the present research was to examine service providers' perception of factors that help or hinder the process of restabilization among mother-headed homeless families.

2. This study compares child welfare supervisors from majority culture state agencies with those of tribal agencies in terms of ethnicity, professionalization, tasks, training needs, and job satisfaction.

3. The purpose of the study was to examine the experiences of victims of spouse abuse with the police and to describe their expectations for police intervention.

4. _____
_____
_____
_____

5. _____

_____

_____

_____

6. _____

_____

_____

_____

Exercise 7

Copy the phrases or sentences from the Introduction section that signal information about method. Search only in Introduction sections, not Method sections.

1. The study reported here, using grounded theory method, explored . . .

2. We conducted a pilot study using focus groups to examine . . .

3. Participants were required to read vignettes varying in degree of . . .

4. _____

_____

5. _____

_____

6. _____

_____

5
Writing the Literature Review

It is time to focus on writing the literature review. This is one of the key sections at the beginning of your paper because it allows the reader to make connections with the research questions and issues. Therefore, a well-focused and careful process to examine published literature is essential. You will remember that the introduction serves to develop the context for the problem you are exploring. A literature review allows you to examine the research question, topic, problem, or issue in greater detail by considering what other people have said about the topic, how they studied it, and what their studies have shown. Reviewing the literature is essential and certainly no easy process. Six steps are involved in the literature review process: specify the topic or questions in searchable terms, locate and access the information, evaluate or assess the information, organize the information, analyze the information, and synthesize the information. Writing the literature review requires you to assess, organize, and synthesize a wide range of retrieved information. This is no small matter.

A frequent assignment for social work students is to write a literature review in a topical area and provide a critique of that literature. The *Publication Manual* says, "Discuss the literature but do not include an exhaustive historical review" (p. 16). Discuss what others have said or reported—what is new, important, or useful. Provide a balance of various points of view by assessing strengths and limitations. And look for news as you integrate all the pieces into a comprehensive picture of the topic. Your instructor will give you specific directions, but whatever these are you need to communicate that you have read and understood the relevant research sufficiently to integrate, replicate, and expand what is known on a specific topic. You should cite each study in your literature review for a specific purpose. For example, you may want to stress method in one and findings in another. You should not exhaustively summarize every article you read. You will provide a paragraph or two on some studies and perhaps only offer a sentence or two about others. As you read each study, critically consider what the research is about and why including it in your literature review is important.

What Has Been Written or Researched?

With the electronic databases currently available, researchers have access to large bodies of literature. This ease of access will test your ability to remain focused on a specific segment of the literature presented. Consider your audience and purpose before writing. This will help you determine both the breadth and depth needed for your literature review. So remember: Be selective and secure a focus. Many articles will be of interest, but you cannot include everything you find in your review of the literature.

If the purpose of your literature review is to demonstrate to the reader that you understand the central issues related to a specific problem area, you will need to review two types of literature: empirical and theoretical. An empirical literature review summarizes past research and draws conclusions from many separate studies. Often this literature review presents a state of the knowledge in an area. Theoretical literature reviews refer to articles that discuss theory, summarize or critique a number of research studies, or provide a general overview of the concepts and constructs related to your topic of interest (Westerfelt & Dietz, 1997). This type of review helps the reader to understand the conceptual framework underlying the problem or issue. The theory informs the reader about how the problem has been defined and provides an understanding of the behavior or problem. It includes assumptions that have come to be accepted and the historical development of the problem. It must also include important and related research. Take note of frequently cited references and obtain these as part of your search strategy.

Refer to Exercise 1 at the end of the chapter

Although it is always best to read and discuss an original source of information, you will find many articles that contain discussions of other authors' work. Recall that we discussed this problem in chapter 3. If you are unable to obtain or have not read the original article or research, you will need to cite the work as a secondary source.

Place the secondary source, but not the original source, in the reference list. Within the body of the text, name the original work and provide the citation for the secondary source.

For example, if you had not read the study by Hartman and Laird that was cited in Carlson, Wallis, and Weeks' (1997) literature review, your citation in the body of the text would read "Hartman and Laird's study (cited in Carlson, Wallis, & Weeks, 1997)."

Reviewing the Empirical Literature

Reviewing what is contained in the empirical research is a necessary step for any student interested in understanding the main findings, trends, research designs, and data analysis methods; areas of debate or controversy; areas of research that have been neglected; and suggestions for additional research. From this understanding you are in a better position to provide the rationale for a current study or the arguments and position taken in your review paper.

To provide a review of several research studies you will need to collect information from each study to compare and contrast. Basic information on each study would include the purpose, theories used to explain phenomena, sample characteristics, methods for obtaining the samples, definitions of theoretical constructs, operational definitions of variables, data collection procedures, and a summary of main findings. Organizing the findings within a framework assists you in understanding similarities and differences. It also facilitates classification, comparisons, and connections—and helps you achieve an overview.

When you attempt to summarize the method of a published study that contains several conditions or several similar experiments with small variations, concentrate on one experiment or condition and describe it clearly. Then you will be able to mention the variations very briefly and they will be clear (Bem, 1995). For example, for a vignette study, you might describe one of the vignettes and then explain that the other groups read vignettes that varied the age of the client or the number of years of experience of the social worker. For a comparison of interventions, describe one intervention and the dependent measure. Then you can briefly note that other groups were identical except for interventions—which you then describe.

It is not usually desirable to note that several experiments were reported and then describe each one. Describe the general method only. Then, as with the description of various groups, you can explain how the variations on the method were accomplished. When you describe results after using this technique for describing the method, you will find it easy to compare the results for each group or experimental variation at the end of your paragraph.

Refer to Exercise 2 at the end of the chapter

You can create a template using the topics outlined above or you can customize a template to best suit your review characteristics. Use the same format for each study in your review.

Here is an important tip: Throw away your highlighters and sharpen your pencils. Take notes! They are easier to access than highlighting when you begin to write. If you really want ease of access, take notes directly on your word processor. Either way, if you quote, include quotation marks and page references in your notes so you won't accidentally plagiarize when you start writing.

Appraising the Literature

As a student you may not feel qualified to assess the quality of the literature you have read. It may ease your mind to know that publications in professional journals have generally been scrutinized by other professionals before appearing in print. This is known as the "peer-review process." Four or five professional peers have evaluated and accepted the importance of the problem, the relevance of the literature cited, the rationale for the hypotheses, the method of collecting and analyzing data, the conclusions drawn from the data and/or the literature review, and the stated limitations of the study. Thus, peer-reviewed articles are submitted to a higher standard of scrutiny than non-peer-reviewed articles such as those in newsletters. Students relatively new to a field are unlikely to improve on the criticisms obtained in the peer-review process. Thus, you don't *have* to find things to criticize (like flaws in the sample section). However, once in awhile you may read something that you think is flawed. And you may even be right. You may politely point this out if you have an appropriate context for the criticism.

When you decide what constitute appropriate sources, keep the peer-review process in mind. Scholars in our field seldom use any other type of material for their literature surveys. Journals published by professional organizations have usually been peer reviewed. When those same organizations produce newsletters and documents designed to educate the public, they are not meant for scholarly citation. However, newsletters often summarize findings that relate to public policy and the articles contain clues that can direct you to original sources—the professional journal articles where these findings were first published. The same goes for newspaper and magazine stories. You may read about some interesting new finding relevant to social work in a trashy or sophisticated source that is meant for the general public. The name of the researcher will be in that article. Use your library database to search out the original journal publication. If the finding was presented at a conference, find out what university the author is affiliated with, use your Web searching skill, and e-mail the author for a copy of the paper.

And speaking of Web searching, let's take a moment to point out some commonsense strategies for deciding when Internet sources are appropriate for your literature review. Most Web pages are created for purposes such as advertising and entertainment (so called "dot com" sites). You would not hesitate to omit such print sources in your literature search. But what about something that looks a bit more authoritative? A good guideline is to be suspicious if there is no author or date on the site. Assume that if you find something interesting with no designated author, you should check the facts in a professional journal. You might get some ideas for search terms from unauthored sites. If you find an author and a date, surf a bit to learn more about the site. There are some Web sites that contain peer reviewed material that has never appeared in print. Web sites that fall into this category will make it easy for you to understand that they are peer reviewed—they are proud of it. These are likely to be "dot org" sites—the likely sponsor is a professional or charitable organization—or "dot edu" sites—sponsored by educational institutions. Sometimes a "dot edu" site is simply the personal Web site of a professor; if so, you cannot trust the material printed there. Professors who use their own Web sites to publish their research have usually tried and failed to have it published in a reputable journal.

When you use your university library databases that provide full-text articles, you can usually limit your search to peer-reviewed articles only. Wilson Omi-File and Proquest, for example, make this very easy. Note that you often have the option to see articles in HTML or printer-friendly format, or page image PDF format. The PDF format exactly reproduces the article as it appears in print, so you can trust page numbers when you quote. You cannot use the HTML version in this way—although it contains all the words in the original print article.

Synthesizing the Literature

Once you have identified the literature that is to appear in your review, you need to decide how to organize the information. Articles may be grouped according to similar purposes, research goals, findings, or similar methodological issues. From these groupings, you can map an outline of the concepts and studies to be presented in your review. Translating the similarities and differences among sources into the language of hypotheses (i.e., statements that provide the basis for further arguments) will assist you in developing the flow of your literature review. Reviewing what the available empirical literature reveals will assist you in understanding the similarities and differences between previous research and current research. This is known as a synthesis of the literature. Reviewing the literature is not simply recounting what has been done in a long list of studies. It requires you to put them together in unique ways that reflect your critical thinking abilities and highlight the patterns that you have noticed across studies. Many critical thinking skills that social workers learn to use with clients are also applicable to writing a literature review. For example, you need to identify similarities and differences; recognize contradictions and inconsistencies; clarify issues, conclusions, and assumptions; evaluate arguments and interpretations; and identify evidence that supports the degree of accuracy of various sources of information.

A common mistake that students make in reviewing the literature is to include only studies or articles that support their perspective. But a good literature review is balanced, and your written presentation of the literature should contain multiple perspectives, including opposing findings and comments regarding the limitations of your own review of the literature.

Let's assume that you have gathered the information from your review of the literature. You have noted patterns across various articles and empirical studies. You have noted the limitations. Now it is time to sift out what is new in all of this. Do the findings in these studies support your study question or hypotheses? How do your findings or analyses apply or relate to your topic of study? If you are preparing to conduct a research study, you must decide what you can apply from the studies reviewed to your own research. It is also wise to consider how you might use the strengths of previous research and how to compensate for the limitations you have noted.

Organizing the Literature Review

After gathering all your notes, it is time to organize them for your review. Stay focused on your purpose and do not let yourself get sidetracked by peripheral issues. Keep in mind the point you are making about each article and study. This will help you write introductory sentences to the paragraphs containing the details. Students sometimes find themselves stringing together ideas or studies without good reason for doing so. When this happens, they introduce paragraphs with phrases such as "Smith (1995) found that . . ." or "Smith (1995) also did a study of . . ." An author-by-author or study-by-study account is common in student writing. But it shows that the student has not made connections among the studies in the review. Thus, *also* is not a good term to use in linking studies together unless you want to make the point that the two researchers did something very similar. Perhaps you have decided to build a case for supporting a theory by adding more evidence. If this is true, then say so. Alternatively, you might prefer to emphasize that one study appears similar to another but an important difference remains and you want to explain it. Knowing *why* you are including a particular study will give you a much better idea of *where* to include it. In this way, your paragraphs will begin with more natural transitions and have appropriately clear topic sentences.

With the purpose of your study in mind, your written review should reflect your intended audience. Is it a review to inform or educate the uninitiated, or is it a review for a scholarly audience? Keep in mind that your literature review will contain new observations and news about the articles you read, so it is wise to refer frequently to the intended audience.

Refer to Exercise 3 at the end of the chapter

Your literature review is not the place for your opinions, although your opinions are implicit in your selection and organization of sources. If you find the sample in an experiment to be very small, you can call attention to that fact only if someone else has found different results with a similar but larger sample. Or perhaps the author has noted a problem in the Discussion section; if so, you then have tacit permission to cite the author's own misgivings. You may speculate about contradictory findings, but once again, be careful not to take a negative tone about the work of either author. Try not to write about what authors *did not do* unless you are contrasting it with what you are about to do or what someone else did. For example, Bradshaw may not have tested middle-aged adults, and Cuvez may not have had a no-treatment control group. You may not mention this just to show off that you noticed. It seldom wins you points with your instructor. If your study contains middle-aged participants, then you can use Bradshaw's results (emphasizing the missing middle-aged group) to provide a rationale for your own hypotheses or design.

Don't forget the rules on verb tense in your literature review. You are reporting on work that has been completed. Therefore, use past tense (found) or present perfect tense (have found). Even your *own* work has already been completed by the time you report the results, so use past tense when you talk about the purpose of your study, the hypotheses, or what the participants had to do. The exception occurs when your introduction concerns a research proposal, which students are often required to write. In this case, the research is clearly not completed. For research proposals, use present and future tense in writing about your study (e.g., "the purpose is" and "the participants will").

Use past tense to describe research findings—your own and those covered in your literature review.

Use Headings

The literature review requires the use of headings. In general, students do not use enough headings in their written presentation of the literature review. Methodological articles or research studies follow APA-style headings. The organization of your review could follow that of any research study: introduction (remember that the overall header "Introduction" is not used), methodology (including how you obtained your sample of articles, inclusion and/or exclusion criteria, etc.), results, and discussion. The results and discussion sections may be combined and subheadings used to highlight your findings. When you just can't think of a good transition sentence for your next paragraph, it may be time to consider breaking your review into sections. If you have a heading for a section, you can avoid that difficult transition sentence; the heading tells the reader where you are going. But don't abuse the help of headings. For example, don't use headings to avoid logical sequencing. Use them to enhance the evidence of your logic.

Here is where an outline will help you. Although most people are taught that it is appropriate to outline a paper before writing it, few people actually do so. We encourage you to try to write an outline, as it helps most writers to focus and organize their thinking. You may find, however, that it is easier to outline your paper *after* you begin to write. Write an outline (if you have not used headings) when you finish your first draft. Be sure to print your draft first; outlining cannot be done from an on-screen manuscript. Outline the paper as it stands. If this proves difficult, you have not done a good job of organizing your paper. The topic sentences should guide you in your outline. If they are missing, this is the time to provide them. Outline *again* after your second draft. If you still can't do it, ask someone else to try it, and if that person also finds your draft difficult to outline, ask why. A good literature review should be easy to outline.

> *If you have not written your paper from an outline, then outline your paper after it is written.*

In the appendixes we have provided examples of outline presentations: a research report/proposal outline (Appendix A) and a theoretical concept review paper outline (Appendix B).

The *Publication Manual* is very explicit about how to organize your manuscript with headings. (Headings are especially useful in the Method section, and we will take them up again in the chapter devoted to that section of your manuscript.) A manuscript may have headings and subheadings. The subheadings may have subheadings of their own, and so on. These are referred to as *levels* of headings. Students' work is likely to have one, two, or three levels of headings. If you have one level, that means that none of your sections has a subsection. Your headings should be centered and important words should begin with uppercase letters:

Here Is an Example of Such a Heading

If you have two levels, that means that your sections have subsections. Your big units are headed as above, centered and containing upper- and lowercase letters. Your subheadings are also in upper- and lowercase letters but they are up against the left margin and italicized. They look like this:

Here Is the Main Heading

Here Is the Subheading

Here is the beginning of the paragraph you will write under this subheading.

Finally, if you have three levels, that is, if your subsections have subsections, everything begins the same way. But your lowest level is indented with your paragraph and only the first letter is uppercase. It ends with a period. All three levels of heads are shown next:

Here Is the Main Heading (Call it A)

Here Is the Subheading for That Section (Call it B)

And here is the heading under that (Call it C). This is the material that you will write under this section. When you have finished writing this material you can start a new section with another heading like C. When that is finished you may wish to do another, or you can go back to the level above it—B. You are even allowed to have another big section we've called A. The *Publication Manual* will take you through steps allowing you to use up to five levels. But don't try this at home!

 **Exercise 1**

Copy phrases that indicate the main topic of a review article.

1. The two most frequently utilized theories for understanding why battered women remain so long in abusive relationships are . . .

2. Twenty-five years of research into juvenile delinquency have provided four constructs that modify aggressive and violent behaviors: . . .

3. _____

_____

_____

4. _____

_____

_____

Exercise 2

Provide the following information from one empirical study.

Author(s) _____

Date of publication _____

Title _____

_____

Source _____

The purpose of the study _____

_____

The theories forming the background of the study _____

_____

_____

_____

Sample characteristics and method for obtaining sample _____

_____

_____

_____

_____

The major constructs in the study _____

_____

_____

How the contructs were operationalized _____

_____

_____

_____

_____

The specific measures used in the study _____

_____

_____

_____

_____

The administration procedures used for data collection _____

_____

_____

_____

_____

_____

The major findings _____

_____

_____

_____

_____

_____

Limitations of the study _____

_____

_____

_____

_____

_____

Exercise 3

Copy phrases that introduce discussion of specific studies under review.

1. In line with these findings . . .

2. Another puzzling aspect of family dynamics is . . .

3. Although Bradshaw's (1995) findings are indications of support for changing court procedures, Cuvez (1996) reaches a different conclusion . . . .

4. The results of the Self-Esteem Ratings Scale are consistent with . . .

5. _____

_____

6. _____

_____

7. _____

_____

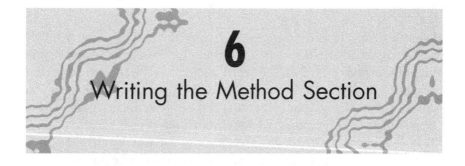

6
Writing the Method Section

The purpose of the Method section is twofold. First, by providing the details of the sample and procedures, you make it possible for other researchers to replicate your study exactly or to make explicit how they are deviating from your procedure. Second, once a reader knows the details of your method, it becomes possible to judge the reliability and validity of your study. When you understand these joint purposes, you are able to make decisions more easily about the level of detail you must achieve.

Organization

It is common for the Method section to be divided into subsections. These will generally include at least a Participants subsection (the term *Subjects* is now reserved for animals) and a Procedure subsection. This usually refers to the administrative aspects of your study or the processes used in administering or implementing the study. Often, the Materials (if special materials are developed or used), the Intervention Description, and the Measures used will be described in separate subsections as parts of the Method section. When archival data (data files that already exist—i.e., you did not need to recruit participants to provide data) are used, you may see a Sample subsection instead of Participants. You are free to decide how subsections can best clarify your work.

The titles for the subsections of the Method section are flexible. Use them to your advantage.

Look at some research articles and copy the subheadings from the Methods section. Note that in editions of the *Publication Manual* before the fourth (1994), the word *subject* was used instead of *participant*. Therefore, in journals printed before this change went into effect, you will find a subsection called *Subjects* rather than *Participants*. In fact, some non-APA journals still accept the term *subjects*. You should use *participants* unless your group did not provide direct consent, as when you observe people engaged in some public activity.

Refer to Exercise 1 at the end of the chapter

Now let's consider the contents of some of these subsections.

Participants

In describing participants who provided data for a study, first indicate how many there were. You must also provide some standard information about them and whatever information is relevant to your particular study. The most basic level of information about participants is age and gender. Report age ranges and mean ages. Elsewhere in your manuscript, standard deviations accompany all means, but this is not the convention when reporting age of participants. Indicate the appropriate unit of measure (e.g., years, months). If you have more than one group of participants, you do not have to report ages for each group unless the groups vary notably or intentionally. But you do have to indicate how many were in each group.

Report age ranges and mean age of participants. Indicate the unit of measure.

Report how many men (or boys) and women (or girls) there were. The *Publication Manual* cautions against the use of the terms *male* and *female* as nouns. You should use *men* and *women* and *girls* and *boys* (high school age and younger) instead. You can use *males* and *females* if the age range includes both children and adults. Otherwise, use *male* and *female* only as adjectives (e.g., female investigator, male clients, male and female adolescents). Do not use *elderly;* substitute *older adults* or *older persons.* Be careful also to use nonbiased labeling of sexual orientation. Preferred terms are *lesbians, gay men, and bisexual men and women.* In the same spirit, do not reduce people to their diagnoses. It is better to write *people with bipolar disorder* than to call them *bipolars.*

Use men and women instead of males and females.

Refer to Exercise 2 at the end of the chapter

Report general information about the nature of the population from which the participants come. For example, they may be students in social work classes at a midwestern university or clients in a Boston social service agency. Note how they were selected. Perhaps they volunteered, answered an advertisement, or were stopped on the street. Do not say that they were "randomly selected" unless they really were. That would mean that you had access to the whole population (of university students, clients at the agency, or people on the street) and actually used a technique to randomly select (e.g., a coin toss, a table of random numbers, or numbers pulled out of a hat) the people you solicited to participate.

Do not write participants were randomly selected when participants volunteered is more accurate.

Refer to Exercise 3 at the end of the chapter

Sometimes people are given something in return for their participation in studies. Undergraduate social work students may get extra credit or may participate as one way to fulfill course requirements. People may be paid money to participate. You must indicate what, if anything, was given to participants in exchange for their help with the study. Otherwise, you may just say they volunteered to participate.

You should specify the race or ethnicity of participants. The *Publication Manual* is specific with regard to which designations are preferred (e.g., *Asian* or *Asian American* rather than *Oriental; Native*

American rather than *American Indian,* but in many cases the specific Indian group or nation would be best). Remember that racial and ethnic group labels are proper nouns and should be capitalized (e.g., *Black* and *White*). Always be sensitive to the changing standards for inoffensive labeling. The *Publication Manual* suggests that you ask your participants about their preferred designations if you are unsure. And remember that "hyphenated Americans" have no hyphens in their spelling: Cuban American, African American, Asian American, and so on. This rule holds even if the labels are used together as a single modifier, for example, Italian American social workers.

Racial and ethnic group labels are proper nouns. Capitalize them.

Often participants in studies come from specific populations relevant to the nature of the study. They share some characteristic of interest. They may be children at certain grade levels, infants born full term, clients with specific problems, people of specific sexual orientation, children of divorced parents, people with specific test score ranges, people above a certain educational level, people of a certain socioeconomic status, and so on.

Refer to Exercise 4 at the end of the chapter

When participants are not randomly assigned to groups but are grouped instead by inherent characteristics, the groups may differ from each other in experimentally undesirable ways. For example, a divorced group may be older than a nondivorced group, or an older adult group may have completed fewer years of school than a middle-aged group. When it is relevant to the research to demonstrate that these other variables have been controlled or that differences have been noted, a researcher will include a statistical analysis of these group differences in the Participants section. Thus, in this section you may find descriptive statistics and/or statistical comparisons of means of such variables as age, education, general health, or verbal ability. Alternatively, this information may be reported in the first section of the Results section of the study.

Statistics may be reported in the Participants section if they describe preexisting differences between groups.

Sometimes participants are randomly assigned to groups, and at other times the grouping factor is based on some characteristic of the participants (e.g., age, gender, occupation, nationality, diagnosis). If the groupings are based on such characteristics, describe the details of this grouping in the Participants section. Do not say "participants were divided into men and women." Choose a phrase indicating your understanding that you have no control over gender and that you merely grouped them accordingly, such as "participants were grouped according to sex." If you randomly assigned participants to groups, it is usually more appropriate to indicate that you did so in your Procedure section.

Descriptive statistics about the participants and/or the analysis of group equivalence may need to be reported. When two or more groups are being compared, it is important to know that the groups do not differ on a number of variables that may affect the outcome of the study. Because most social work research does not allow for random selection, researchers cannot make the assumption that any two groups of people will have a similar distribution of characteristics. The question of which characteristics to assess can often be found in the literature. For example, if previous research suggested that the level of physical abuse reported by rural women tended to be more severe than that reported by urban women, residence status is an important variable that is not of interest in certain studies. If your groups are not equivalent on important variables, then you may need to use specific statistical procedures to control for the effect of this difference.

After you have made relevant information about participants clear to the reader, begin to use these more descriptive terms instead of referring to them as participants (e.g., the young and older adults, the children, the students). Alternatively, you can use terms that describe the nature of their participation (e.g., respondents, perceivers, raters).

When some participants do not complete the research tasks, it is necessary to indicate how many dropped out and why. For example, some adults fail to come back for a second session; some people may fail to meet certain criteria after testing has begun. When surveys are mailed to participants, some are not returned and others are returned as addressee unknown. Indicate the number of surveys mailed out and what percentage of the surveys was actually completed. When participants do not complete a study, avoid reporting that they *failed* to do so. Say they *did not* do so.

Refer to Exercise 5 at the end of the chapter

Researchers are expected to treat participants in accordance with the ethical guidelines established by the profession. Sometimes a sentence to this effect appears toward the end of the Participants section. Your instructor may give you specific guidance about this if it is expected. Such a statement is often not included in a published article because for many journals, authors are required to attest to its truth in the cover letters they submit with their manuscripts. This requirement would appear in the instructions to authors printed somewhere in the journals. Thus, compliance with these guidelines can be assumed for all studies published in those journals even though the articles do not attest to it in each case.

Materials and Measures

Materials in this sense usually refers to printed or recorded materials. Audiotapes, videotapes, vignettes, curriculum content, manuals, and computer programs would be included in this subsection of your study. When describing materials, allow readers to understand the task participants are asked to perform from the point of view of the participants while also providing enough information for replication. You may be using materials bought or borrowed (with appropriate citations) from other authors, or you may have constructed them yourself.

When you have used published tests or questionnaires you may list them in the section on Materials or you may create a Measures subsection. Give the author and year as you would any citation. Indicate what the test measures. Try to tie the terms to your Introduction section, in which you have noted how you operationalized your dependent measures (e.g., Gabor, Thomlison, & Hudson's [1999] Family Assessment Screening Inventory [FASI] was used to measure problems in families). If you have reliability and validity information that pertains to your population, include those references as well. Indicate the meaning of the score (e.g., scores range from 15 to 45 with higher scores indicating more severe problems). Use past tense to describe what your participants did (e.g., the participants were asked to place a mark on the letter . . .) and present tense to describe enduring characteristics of a test (e.g., the test measures family functioning in specific domains).

Questionnaires and tests you devise yourself should be explained more fully. In addition to all the information suggested for published tests, it is helpful to provide sample questions in the body of the paper and the complete test or questionnaire in an appendix.

Researchers often construct scales that require participants to choose a numerical response, for example, from 1 to 5. These may be referred to as Likert scales or Likert-type scales. The high and low points (1 and 5 in the current example) are called the *anchors* of the scale. In writing about scales, use a hyphen between the number and the word *point* (e.g., 5-point scale), and italicize the anchors (e.g., *never* and *always*). Usually, the points between the anchors (e.g., *sometimes*) are not labeled, but if they are, these labels must also be italicized.

Italicize the anchors of a scale.

Refer to Exercise 6 at the end of the chapter

Sometimes researchers use materials that are not measures, such as passages to write or read, lists to check, videotapes to watch, and so on. As with measures, these materials may have been developed by others and you used them as originally designed, or you modified them, or you may have developed the materials specifically for your study. Be sure to indicate the source accordingly. In describing these materials, follow the rules of explaining the task from the point of view of the participant and giving enough detail for replication (perhaps in an appendix, table, or figure).

Refer to Exercise 7 at the end of the chapter

It is tricky to describe materials that vary by intervention condition before you have described the actual procedure. If the design and materials are interrelated (e.g., different word lists for different groups, vignettes whose clients vary by intervention group, etc.), remember that you are under no obligation to have a separate Materials section. You can use a Design and Materials section if this happens. In this section you explain how many groups there were, how participants were assigned to the groups, and what the independent variable(s) were that controlled the grouping. Then the reader will be ready for the information that each group received slightly different materials. Remember, a reader can become confused when there are several conditions that differ primarily according to the materials used, especially if you describe the materials before describing the conceptual differences among the conditions. Some authors decide to include the description of materials within the Procedure section—or even after the Procedure section—to solve this type of writing problem. It may be better to leave out a special Materials section rather than confuse a reader with descriptions of sets of materials for various intervention groups before you have explained the purpose of the groups.

In some studies, you will find a few paragraphs in the Method section that define important variables, both dependent and independent, and indicate how these variables have been implemented. It is best to assume that the reader of the study will not know what you mean by certain constructs unless you explain each one.

Refer to Exercise 8 at the end of the chapter

Procedure

The *Publication Manual* instructs that the purpose of the Procedure section is to "tell the reader *what* you did and *how* you did it" (p. 20). There are two points of view that you must be aware of in this part of the manuscript: the researcher's and the participant's. Use the researcher's point of view to describe how the experiment was organized, and use the participant's point of view to describe the task.

Start with the organization of your study. What were the conditions? Did everyone participate in every condition (within-subjects design) or were people grouped in some way (between-subjects design)? Were they grouped by some previously noted characteristic or randomly assigned? (Please remember that people are assigned to conditions; conditions are *not* assigned to people.)

Provide names for your groups or conditions that help the reader remember the key distinguishing features. For example, the *alcohol information group* and the *no information group* are better designations than *Group A* and *Group B*. Feel free to give a short name or abbreviation (acronyms are good) to a group after describing it. The alcohol information group might be the AI group, and the no-information group might be the NI group. Be sure to refer to the group consistently by that term throughout the manuscript. Note that the names of groups and conditions are not capitalized unless they have been given letter or number names (Group A; the alcohol information group). Abbreviations are usually written in all uppercase letters (the AI group). Keep in mind that abbreviations should help, not confuse, the reader. So don't overdo it.

Capitalize the name of the condition only if the name is a letter or a number.

Refer to Exercise 9 at the end of the chapter

Be careful with the terms *group* and *condition*. Although they are related and almost equivalent in the researcher's mind, they are not linguistically equivalent. People are in groups, but they are not in conditions. Groups can perform tasks, but conditions cannot. It is often best to use the word *participants* as the subject of your sentence, for example, "Depending on condition, participants were told that they would hear A or see B."

Use the term condition carefully. People are assigned to conditions, not the other way around. People can't be in conditions, and conditions can't perform tasks.

Once you have explained how the study was organized, explain the task the participants were asked to perform. Start with the general nature of the task, and then give details that apply to all of the groups. Later, explain how the groups differed. Use the participant as the focus rather than the investigator. That is, state that the participants read, rated, completed, listened to, or watched rather than say the investigator gave the participant something to read, rate, complete, listen to, or watch.

Refer to Exercise 10 at the end of the chapter

Finally, explain the method of scoring if it is not obvious. If a summary score was calculated and used for data analysis, explain how that was done.

Remember Your Audience

When in doubt about what level of detail to use, always assume that your audience is composed of experienced readers. Do not tell them the following:

1. *How you randomized.* Just say that participants were randomly assigned to conditions or treatment groups. Don't say that you used a table of random numbers. If additional details are relevant (e.g., equal numbers of men and women in each group), state them briefly.

2. *How instructions were phrased.* Do not say participants were told to complete the questions as fast as they could but to try not to make mistakes. State that instructions stressed speed and accuracy.

3. *How answers were managed.* Simply state that answers or responses were recorded verbatim.

4. *How ordinary materials were handled.* Do not explain that participants used pencils to write their answers and that they gave the answer sheets to the investigator when they were finished. Just describe the answer sheets.

Don't tell readers more than they need to know. Assume common sense and familiarity with research methodology.

 **Exercise 1**

Look at some research articles and copy the subheadings from the Methods section.

1. Participants

   Measures and Materials

   Procedures

2. Setting and Sample

   Data Collection Procedures

   Measures

3. _____

   _____

   _____

   _____

4. _____

   _____

   _____

   _____

5. _____

   _____

   _____

   _____

Exercise 2

From the Participants or Subjects sections of research articles, copy sentences that indicate number, age, and gender information of participants.

1. One hundred women aged 35 to 55 (M age = 40.1 years) participated.

2. Participants were 32 social work undergraduates (23 women and 9 men) at the University of Alabama (mean age = 23.7 years).

3. The sample consisted of 17 male and 18 female children of divorced parents and their custodial parents. Children ranged in age from 5 to 7 years (M = 6.3), and parents ranged in age from 23 to 45 years (M = 37.1).

4. _____
    _____
    _____

5. _____
    _____
    _____

6. _____
    _____
    _____

Exercise 3

Copy sentences or phrases that indicate the general nature of the population of participants.

1. One hundred women 35 years or older living in rural communities in West Virginia agreed to participate.

2. The participants were 435 tenth-grade students from two urban high schools who completed an anonymous questionnaire and were paid $10.

3. All children were of middle to upper-middle socioeconomic status.

4. _____

    _____

    _____

5. _____

    _____

    _____

6. _____

    _____

    _____

Exercise 4

Copy examples of specific descriptions of participants and the criteria used to select them or the characteristics by which they were grouped. As you do this, think about why these characteristics were noted by the researchers. The characteristics noted for this exercise are more narrowly defined than for the previous one.

1. There were 28 participants who demonstrated disruptive behaviors in the classroom and 13 participants who were diagnosed with ADHD.

2. The sample consisted of 100 nonprofit organizations dedicated to violence prevention in schools that either (a) used only trained professional(s) from their agency ($n = 30$); (b) used one trained staff person plus trained volunteers ($n = 30$); or (c) trained classroom teachers to deliver the program ($n = 40$).

3. _____

_____

_____

_____

_____

_____

4. _____

_____

_____

_____

_____

_____

5. _____

_____

_____

_____

_____

_____

Exercise 5

Copy sentences that refer to dropouts from studies or survey return rates.

1. Data were eliminated from 129 participants who completed less than 85% of the questions and from 46 who met criteria for excessive inconsistent responses.

2. Of the initial 300 participants, 45 dropped out of the group before the final session and 22 did not complete the 3-month follow-up testing. Data from these participants are not included in any of the analyses.

3. _____

_____

_____

_____

4. _____

_____

_____

_____

Exercise 6

Find descriptions of scales. Copy sentences and phrases that indicate the number of points on the scale and the labels or anchors.

  1. Test A uses a 5-point Likert scale with responses ranging from 1 _(almost never or never true)_ to 5 _(almost always or always true)._

  2. Participants indicated their responses on a 3-point rating scale (1 = _never,_ 2 = _sometimes,_ and 3 = _always_).

  3. Responses range from 1 _(not at all true of me)_ to 5 _(always true of me)._

  4. _____

_____

  5. _____

_____

  6. _____

_____

 **Exercise 7**

Look for articles that display samples of the study's materials in a table or a figure. Copy the sentence that refers the reader to the material (table, figure, or appendix) and that indicates the type of material displayed.

1. The participants' family relationships were explored with three questions, displayed in Table 1.

2. A modified scale suitable for the Hispanic population was developed from Hudson's existing measure of family problems. Sample items are presented in Figure 2.

3. _____

   _____

4. _____

   _____

Exercise 8

Find and copy definitions of variables. Indicate whether the variable is dependent or independent.

1. For the purpose of this study, self-disclosure is defined as . . . (independent variable).

2. Sense of humor was measured by Curly and Moe's (1968) Laugh Scale (dependent variable).

3. Belonging was measured by participants' ratings of the family photographs on a 9-point scale (dependent variable).

4. _____

   _____

5. _____

   _____

6. _____

_____

 **Exercise 9**

Copy sentences that contain information about conditions or groups.

1. Half of the participants were randomly assigned to meet in face-to-face groups (FTF), and the other half watched video-tapes (VT)

2. Participants were assigned to one of the four conditions of the 2 (normative vs. at-risk) × 2 (8-week program vs. 16-week program) factorial design.

3. Each participant saw one of the three taped interviews with the family.

4. _____

_____

_____

5. _____

_____

_____

6. _____

_____

_____

Exercise 10

From Procedure sections, copy sentences that describe tasks that participants performed.

1. Each participant attended the 3-hour violence prevention workshop.

2. Participants read the booklet on how to complete an application for low-income housing.

3. Participants labeled the person in each vignette as deserving or not deserving of government assistance.

4. _____

    _____

5. _____

    _____

6. _____

    _____

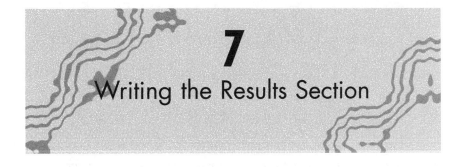

7
Writing the Results Section

The Results section should contain the summary of your findings, including the results of statistical analyses. This section should be written in a predictable form. Report the statistical tests of your hypotheses in the order in which the hypotheses were originally presented. Do not give in to the temptation to start with the finding you like best or to end with one that supports your favorite hypothesis. Lead the reader through your analyses in the most logical order, not the most exciting. Do not discuss which hypotheses were supported and which were not. It is fine to use the same sentence format for every result that involves the same type of statistic rather than to vary your sentence construction for its own sake.

State results in the order that corresponds to the order of the hypotheses as presented in the introduction.

Statistics

In this section, the *Publication Manual* is very specific about what kind of information to report for each analysis. For *t* tests, *F* tests, and chi-square tests, include the numerical value obtained for the statistic, degrees of freedom, and probability level. Reporting confidence levels is also strongly recommended. For *F* tests, also include the mean square of the error term *(MSE)*. Indicate the direction of effect; for example, *Group A scored significantly higher than Group B is*

better than *the scores of the two groups were significantly different.*
Follow this information with the actual *t*-test result. You must report
actual means and standard deviations (or some other measure of variability) whenever you report that means differed. These may be provided in a table.

> *Whenever an effect is significant, report the direction of that effect.*

Students are usually required to report a bit more information
than the researcher reporting in a journal. For example, after a *t*-test
result, you must indicate whether it was one-tailed or two-tailed.
Also, you will have to include statistical values for all of your results,
even the nonsignificant ones. Please note that the word *insignificant*
is not a technical term and does not belong in your paper. If you need
to say that the result was not significant, use the word *nonsignificant.*

> *Use* nonsignificant *rather than* insignificant *if an analysis does not yield an acceptable level of significance.*

The *Publication Manual* advises that you report exact *p* values
provided by statistical packages. The main thing to remember when
reporting probability is to use the *less than* symbol and the *equal*
symbol appropriately. If the value comes from a table, use the *less
than* symbol (e.g., $p < .05$); if it comes from a statistical package, use
the *equal* symbol (e.g., $p = .023$). But note this exception: If the computer printout indicates a probability level of .000, you should write
$p < .001$. *P* values cannot be zero, so .000 on a printout indicates that
the probability has been rounded off. The real probability may have
been .0000071. If you drop the last zero in the value on your printout and replace it with a 1, and then you claim that $p < .001$, you
have made an accurate statement (.0000071 *is* less than .001).

Note that *t* test is hyphenated when it is used as a compound
adjective (as in *t*-test results), but not otherwise. Note also that statistical symbols are italicized.

Refer to Exercise 1 at end of the chapter

Note that Greek letters are not italicized. Degrees of freedom and sample size are included in parentheses. Degrees of freedom are included for most other statistics as well, but sample sizes are not. You are also required to report cell frequencies, but these often appear on a table.

Refer to Exercise 2 at end of the chapter

A report of analysis of variance results usually contains the abbreviation ANOVA, for analysis of variance. The rule for abbreviations is the same for the Results section as for the rest of your study. Introduce the abbreviation in parentheses the first time you use the term, then use only the abbreviation thereafter. If you do not use the term a second time in the manuscript, do not introduce the abbreviation at all. The abstract does not count as part of the manuscript for this rule.

Introduce abbreviations in parentheses and use the abbreviations rather than the full term thereafter.

Usually the *F* test is reported for the ANOVA. Students have varying degrees of familiarity with ANOVA results. Undergraduates are likely to have experience with one-way analyses and analyses using two independent variables. Therefore, these will be the focus here.

If you compared three or more means in a one-way analysis, report the results using the term *one-way analysis of variance.* Remember that a significant finding indicates that *at least one mean was different.* Because this finding lacks precision, authors usually do planned or post hoc tests on these means. Planned comparisons are reported as such. Post hoc tests are usually named (e.g., Tukey or Scheffe) and a significance level targeted prior to the calculation. You are also expected to provide cell means, cell standard deviations, and an estimate of the pooled within-cell variance. These often appear on a table.

Refer to Exercise 3 at the end of the chapter

Analyses with two independent variables require the reporting of main effects and interactions. The safest way to report these is either with both main effects preceding the interaction or with the interaction first. Do not report one main effect, then the interaction, then the other main effect. Again, as with *t* tests, if you say a main effect was significant (e.g., "The main effect of color was significant"), take the opportunity to say right at that time what the direction of the effect was (e.g., "The main effect of color was significant, with the blue-pencil group scoring higher than the green, *F* . . . ")

Interactions generally leave you two choices for phrasing: (a) "The interaction between age and instructional condition was significant, F . . . " or (b) "The Age × Instructional Condition interaction was significant, F . . . " Capitalization rules are somewhat unexpected: main effects are lowercase, but interactions are capitalized.

Capitalize interaction terms but not main effects.

Do not be concerned that you have several sentences in a row with the same structure. Readers will not be put off by this; rather, they will appreciate the clarity.

Refer to Exercise 4 at the end of the chapter

Correlation results require the correlation coefficient *(r)* and the p value. Reporting correlation results can be a preposition nightmare. These are acceptable statements of correlation:

X correlated significantly with Y

X and Y were significantly correlated.

The correlation between X and Y was significant. The correlation of X and Y was significant.

Correlations among X, Y, and Z were computed.

The correlation of X with Y was significant.

Refer to Exercise 5 at the end of the chapter

You must report means and standard deviations, but you do have some choice as to where to do so. They may be presented in a table, in the text, or in parentheses right after the statistic that compared them.

When statistical analyses are used to compare means, provide all relevant means and standard deviations in the text or in a table, but not in both.

The *Publication Manual* strongly advises authors to provide effect size estimates as well as significance tests. A few authors routinely report η^2 (Eta squared) with F test results: $F(1, 115) = 623.16$, $MSE = .01$, $p < .01$, $\eta^2 = .83$. There are various effect size estimates to choose from, and your instructor will guide you.

Refer to Exercise 6 at the end of the chapter

Likewise, authors are encouraged to report power estimates, particularly when they wish to discuss results that do not achieve statistical significance.

Refer to Exercise 7 at the end of the chapter

The *Publication Manual* advises that tables should be used sparingly because they are inconvenient for readers and expensive to publish. Your professor may instruct you to present certain findings in tabular fashion to give you practice. If the decision is up to you, use the *Publication Manual's* guideline that a table with only three numbers probably presents data that could more conveniently be provided in the text. When preparing a table, consult the *Publication Manual* for directions. The APA guidelines for tables are unique and complex. Although some basic rules are presented here, if you prepare a table, consult the *Publication Manual* for further directions. Another good source is Nicol and Pexman's (1999) *Presenting Your Findings,* a book published by the APA that can guide you in formatting tables.

Tables should be numbered with arabic numerals in the order that they are mentioned in the text. In addition, tables have titles that give an indication of which variables are contained in them but without duplicating all of the words labeling rows and columns. For example, *Mean Happiness Ratings for All Conditions* is better than *Mean Happiness Ratings and Standard Deviations for Fun Condition, Pain Condition, and Control Condition.* Locate table number in the upper left corner of the page and place the title, italicized, below it.

Next, consider the words identifying the rows and columns. Every column needs a heading, even the one on the far left that probably contains words (e.g., independent variables) rather than numbers. Often column headings are organized into several layers. The top layer (called column spanners) is the most general division of the material, for example, the name of the independent variable. Under that is a further division, for example, each level of that variable.

Under that may be yet another division, for example, the type of information being reported. A means table may be organized like this:

Table 1	*Means for Age Groups as a Function of Instructional Condition*					
	Instructional Condition					
	Verbal		Written		Control	
Age Group	*M*	*SD*	*M*	*SD*	*M*	*SD*

The means in this table can easily be compared across age groups or across instructional conditions. Align columns carefully with plenty of space between columns. Note that APA style tables have horizontal lines separating each row of headers but they have no vertical lines separating columns. Tables also end with a line spanning the last row of data. Under that line you may find additional notes explaining abbreviations or symbols and also footnotes relating to *p* values. Everything in the table is double-spaced, even the lines spanning the columns. Many types of tables (e.g., means tables, correlation tables, ANOVA tables) have a basic format and you should look for models in journals that contain the type of data you wish to present. Nicol and Pexman (1999) also provide many models for these and other tables.

Contrary to what you might expect, tables are placed at the end of your manuscript, *after* the References section.

Refer to Exercise 8 at the end of the chapter

If you do use a table, you must refer the reader to it and indicate what will be found there. This is a good time to think about verbs and sentence subjects again. If a table is to be the grammatical subject of a sentence, just what can it *do?* Do tables *contain* numbers? Do they *display* them? Perhaps. Alternatively, the contents of the table may be the grammatical subject, and then you must figure out what relationship the contents have to the table. Are numbers *on* a table or *in* a table?

Refer to Exercise 9 at the end of the chapter

Graphs can be used to illustrate patterns in your results. They are often used to present statistical interactions. Be aware that all illustrations other than tables are called *Figures,* and their titles appear on a page of their own, entitled *Figure Captions.* All figure captions (but not table titles) appear on this one page, which comes before the figures themselves. All of this is found *after* any tables you have included.

The order for backmatter in your manuscript is Reference, Tables, Figure Captions, Figures

Line graphs and bar graphs are the most common in journals. It is best to produce your graphs with a graphics program that allows a degree of customization. That way you'll be able to follow a lot of very specific APA guidelines, a few of which are presented here. The independent variable is plotted on the x axis and the dependent variable on the y axis. The y axis should be shorter than the x axis (the y axis is often about two thirds the length of the x axis). The axes must be labeled and the unit of measure must be included in the label.

For a line graph, differentiate lines by differentiating plot points. Use clear open and solid circles and triangles as plot points. Lines should all be solid black rather than dashed or dotted. For a bar graph, use simple shading techniques to distinguish between sets of bars. White (no shading) and black are preferable to grays and stripes. If you need a third shade, use diagonal stripes. Do not use color for graphs.

Place a legend inside the graph area. Do not label the lines themselves in a line graph; explain the meanings of the shapes of the plot points or the shadings of the bars in the legend. As with tables, figures are numbered consecutively in the order in which they are referred to in the body of the manuscript. Write the figure number lightly with a pencil (e.g., Figure 1) on the top right front of the page containing each graph, and write the word *top* on the back of the page to show which way is up. Also write the manuscript page header on the back. There is no title except on the figure caption page.

To find the rules for graphs, look under Figures *in the index of the* Publication Manual.

Refer to Exercise 10 at the end of the chapter

Refer to all tables and figures at least once in the body of the paper.

Even if you have decided to list means and standard deviations in the text as a way to avoid the difficulties of referring to tables and figures, you are not off the hook yet. You face the decisions of where to put them and how to refer to them. You can put them after the statistic that indicates they are significantly different from each other. If there are two means, use the word *respectively* to indicate order: "Mean scores for administrators and supervisors were 6.10 (SD = 0.43) and 5.12 (SD = 0.23), respectively." Do not forget standard deviations. You can also squeeze this information into the sentence that reports a *t*-test result by using parentheses. You should use abbreviations for mean *(M)* and standard deviation *(SD)* when they are in parentheses: "Administrators (M = 6.10, SD = 0.43) scored significantly higher than supervisors (M = 5.12, SD = 0.23), t . . . " Always indicate what the mean refers to (e.g., mean ratings, mean scores, mean number correct).

Refer to Exercise 11 at the end of the chapter

Useful Rules

1. Letter symbols (e.g., N, p) are italicized.

2. Greek letters are not italicized.

3. Letters that are abbreviations (e.g., M, SD) should be used only in parentheses. In the narrative, use the word (e.g., mean, standard deviation).

4. Use the symbol for percent (%) whenever it is preceded by a numeral.

5. Use spaces between symbols and within equations as if each term were a word (e.g., $p < .05$).

6. Use numerals for 10 and above, words for nine and below. *Exceptions:*

   a. Never begin a sentence with a numeral. Look up spellings for numbers in the dictionary and pay attention to hyphen use.

b. Use numerals below 10 if they are grouped for comparison with numerals above 10 (e.g., 3 out of 14 trials).

c. Use numerals below 10 in an abstract.

7. Use metric units unless the nonmetric is very familiar (e.g., 3 × 5 cards). In this case put the metric equivalent in parentheses.

8. Use a 0 before a decimal point when the value of a number is less than 1, unless it can *never* be more than 1 (e.g., levels of significance, proportions, correlation coefficients).

9. Rounding off: use two decimal places when reporting inferential statistics and, in general, *p* values. For means, use two decimal places as long as relevant differences can be seen with two decimal places. Otherwise, try to rescale, for example, converting centimeters to millimeters.

10. Abbreviations for any measurement you are likely to need are listed in the *Publication Manual.* Note that most, but not all, abbreviations for units of measurement are neither capitalized nor followed by a period. Leave a space between the numeral and the abbreviated unit of measurement.

11. The plural of *analysis* is *analyses.*

12. *Between* is used for two things: Correlations *between* two variables. *Among* is used for three or more: Correlations were computed *among* three variables.

13. Word your sentences so that statistical results are *not* in parentheses. Many statistical results contain parentheses of their own (containing degrees of freedom, for example). Set off these statistical results with commas instead.

14. Do not use mathematical symbols in your sentences as if they were verbs. For example, the following is incorrect: The number of boys = 17. Write out the word *equal* if you really must write a sentence that uses it. The word *was* works well here. Use the mathematical symbols inside parentheses.

15. Common fractions are expressed in words (e.g., one half of the sample, three fourths of the divorced couples) and others are expressed as numerals (e.g., 3 1/2 sessions).

Exercise 1

Copy sentences that contain *t*-test results.

1. Overall mean ratings of self-esteem did not differ as a function of age group, *t*(49) = .03, *ns* (*M* = 27.12 for 60–69 years old and *M* = 28.50 for 50–59 years old).

2. There was a tendency for managers to rate themselves as more approachable than did their staff, *t*(50) = 12.31, *p* < .01.

3. Independent sample one-tailed *t* tests showed that women scored significantly higher than men on knowledge of abuse and violence at both pretest, *t*(29) = 22.41, *p* = .021, and at posttest, *t*(29) = 19.33, *p* = .032.

4. _____

   _____

   _____

   _____

5. _____

   _____

   _____

   _____

6. _____

   _____

   _____

   _____

Exercise 2

Copy sentences that contain chi-square results. Note that Greek letters are not italicized.

1. Chi square χ^2 difference between continuity on mutual versus unidirectional social network relationships = 19.2, *p* < .001.

2. There was a significant relationship, $\chi^2(1, N = 31) = 10.4$, $p <$ .01, between the type of maltreatment (physical or sexual) and whether the child demonstrated internalized or externalized behavior problems.

3. _____

_____

_____

4. _____

_____

_____

Exercise 3

Copy sentences from Results sections that report one-way ANOVAs. If planned comparisons or post hoc tests were done, include those sentences.

1. We analyzed case manager judgments to terminate services using a one-way ANOVA. Participants relied on foster-parent ratings most frequently, followed by therapist ratings, and teacher ratings least frequently, $F(2,100) = 21.3$, $MSE = 7.95$, $p = .004$. See Table 1 for cell means.

2. A one-way ANOVA with diagnosis as the independent variable was conducted. Differences were found for age at onset, $F(2,98) = 7.69$, $p = .008$. Post hoc Duncan's Multiple-Range Tests ($p < .05$) revealed that those with nongeneralized social phobia were significantly older than clients with generalized social phobia, with or without avoidant personality disorder (APD).

3. _____

_____

_____

_____

4. _____

_____

_____

_____

Exercise 4

Find sentences that report 2 × 2 ANOVA results. Copy what you find, including main effects and interactions.

1. We examined mean posttest scores on knowledge of violence prevention for intervention and control groups using a 2 (gender) × 2 (condition) analysis of variance (ANOVA). Overall, male students scored lower than female students, $F(1,62) = 60.51$, $MSE = 27.74$, $p < .0001$. Males in the control group on average scored lower than males in the intervention group, $F(1,62) = 40.3$, $MSE = 16.21$, $p < .05$. The Gender × Condition interaction was significant, $F(1,62) = 29.1$, $MSE = 2.20$, $p < .01$.

2. An analysis of variance performed on these data yielded the following results: group, $F(1,50) = 18.1$, $MSE = 3.21$, $p < 05$; level of income, $F(1,50) = 21.4$, $MSE = 32.81$, $p < .01$. The Group × Level of Income interaction was not significant.

3. _____

_____

_____

_____

_____

_____

4. _____

_____

_____

_____

_____

_____

5. _____

_____

_____

_____

_____

_____

Exercise 5

Copy sentences containing correlation results.

1. The correlation between level of education and use of domestic abuse shelter services was not significant, $r = -.17$.

2. The correlation between age and use of postshelter services was unreliable ($r = .06$), whereas the correlation between levels of physical abuse reported and use of postshelter services was significant ($r = .51$, $p = .003$).

3. _____

_____

_____

_____

4. _____

_____

_____

_____

5. _____

_____

_____

_____

Exercise 6

Copy a sentence containing effect size results.

1. We calculated the effect size of video recording of interviews (versus the audio-taped baseline) using Eta squared as the estimate of effect size, $\eta^2 = .63$.

2. The effect size (η^2) was .76.

3. _____

_____

_____

Exercise 7

Look for an example of power analysis.

1. The . . . was not significant, $F(2, 201) = 0.03$, $p > .05$; the power to detect this effect at alpha = .01 was greater than .95.

2. _____

_____

_____

Exercise 8

Find two tables displaying data you understand. Copy the titles of the tables and the headers.

1. Title: _____

Column headers: _____

_____

_____.

2. Title: _____

Column headers: _____

_____

Exercise 9

Find out now just what acts tables can legally perform. Copy sentences from Results sections that refer readers to tables.

1. Table 3 presents correlations . . .

2. Table 3 indicates frequencies . . .

3. Table 4 summarizes the results of the regression analysis.

4. Mean scores appear in Table 4.

5. _____

6. _____

7. _____

Exercise 10

Copy sentences from Results sections that refer readers to figures.

1. Inspection of Figure 3 indicates . . .

2. As can be seen in Figure 2, . . .

3. Figure 1 illustrates . . .

4. _____

5. _____

Exercise 11

Copy sentences from Results sections that contain information about means and standard deviations.

1. A post hoc test showed that children in foster homes (*M* = 100.00, *SD* = 10.13) and children from single-parent-headed homes (*M* = 101.30, *SD* = 8.45) had significantly higher rates of depression than did children from two-parent-headed homes (*M* = 48.15, *SD* = 7.02).

2. Male managers had, on average, more days absent from work than female managers (male: *M* = 8.35 days, *SD* = 0.83; female: *M* = 6.42 days, *SD* = 0.65).

3. Recent parolees reported a greater number of attended AA meetings in the preceding week than did those who had completed their parole (*M*s = 4.2 and 1.6, respectively).

4. _____

    _____

    _____

    _____

5. _____

    _____

    _____

    _____

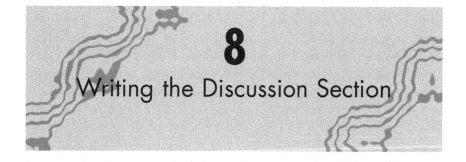

8
Writing the Discussion Section

The Discussion section contains two types of material. The first can be called *inevitable*. It is inevitable that the results will be evaluated in terms of the research questions and/or hypotheses generated in the Introduction. Each statistical analysis was done in an effort to answer one of these questions or test one of these hypotheses. The results of these analyses have been reported in the Results section. In the Discussion section, you must, inevitably, indicate which analyses lead to what answers, or which analyses support or do not support which hypotheses. When hypotheses are supported, you will then, inevitably, refer to the theory or theories that generated those hypotheses. When hypotheses are not supported, you will inevitably admit it, and look back to the method and/or the theory for enlightenment. It should be clear that the inevitable part could be written by anyone who really understood the introduction and results.

The second type of material found in the Discussion section is *creative*, and the creative part can only be written by you. This type of creativity is the type that characterizes the creative researcher, not the poet. You need to step back mentally from your findings and think about what else *might* be interesting about them. If hypotheses are supported, are there other explanations that a creative thinker might come up with besides the happy thought that your hypotheses are simply perfect? In the case of hypotheses that are not supported, what possible explanations exist? Would it be reasonable to make a minor adjustment in the hypothesis in the light of a given result, or are there confounds in the method? Here we are not talking about technical problems that result from undergraduate foul-ups, but real methodological issues that might interfere with the results of the most sophisticated laboratory crew. If your results are entirely unexpected (perhaps significant but in the wrong direction), you can bring in literature you have not mentioned in the introduction to place these unexpected findings in a new context. Most of the literature you refer to in the inevitable part of the Discussion section should have been mentioned in the introduction, but there are exceptions in the creative part. Remember the conceptual difference between past and present tense as it relates to discussion of your research. Your study is over; your results have been analyzed. Reference to what you and your participants did and what you found is always in the past. Statements about human behavior in general are in the present. The implications of your study should be discussed in the present tense. As a result of these directives, your discussion is likely to be primarily in the present tense: results *support* the hypothesis; limitations of the study *are;* findings *contribute* to the literature; results *suggest;* findings *support* the findings of other researchers; performance on these measures *involves.*

Use past tense to describe your results and present tense for statements about human behavior in general.

Refer to Exercises 1 and 2 at the end of the chapter

The *Publication Manual* provides less guidance for the format of the Discussion section than for the other sections. And because it is more creative and freewheeling than the other sections, students sometimes have difficulty knowing when they have written enough. They sometimes resort to noting trivial shortcomings (e.g., not enough participants) and overbroad applications (e.g., that the study should help teachers of students with learning disabilities). However, it is possible to overlay a format of three unofficial sections on most fairly short discussions. We will call them (a) a discussion of the results; (b) implications for theory, research, and/or practice; and (c) limitations of the study and directions for future research. Remember that these conceptualizations are used here as guidelines and do not necessarily signal subheadings for your use.

Discussion of the Results

The Discussion section should begin with an assessment of the results of your main hypothesis. Usually, the entire hypothesis is restated in a sentence concerning its support or nonsupport. You should remind yourself at this point that your study was designed to test a hypothesis, not a theory. A theory probably led to the hypothesis, and support of many such hypotheses lends support to the theory, but you must first deal with the hypotheses in your discussion. Recall that some studies are designed not to test hypotheses that imply direction of effect, but to answer questions, describe characteristics, assess relationships, and so on. When this is the case, the word *hypothesis* will be missing from the first sentence of the discussion; there will, however, be some reference to the purpose of the study as it relates to the statistical analyses. Remember, studies do not *prove* or *confirm* hypotheses. The best way to convert the inferential statistic in your results into plain English for your discussion is with the word *support* or the phrase *fail to support*.

Start your discussion by referring to the main hypothesis. Indicate which statistical result appears to support it or fails to support it. Be sure to discuss the results of each of the analyses reported in the Results section.

Refer to Exercises 3, 4, 5, and 6 at the end of the chapter

You must acknowledge negative results. What can you do with results that fail to support your hypothesis? In the light of these results, you might reconsider the theory. What would be the ramifications of adopting a weaker version of the theory, or, more extreme, of abandoning the theory? Perhaps your failure to extend a previous finding sheds light on the population to which it can reasonably be extended.

Refer to Exercise 7 at the end of the chapter

Implications for Theory, Research, and/or Practice

Implications are the logical consequences and the larger significance of the outcome. If hypotheses are supported, implications are inevitable and should flow directly from a well-written introduction. The logical consequence of a supported hypothesis is a supported theory. This in itself is the larger significance of the outcome. The introduction will have made plain why this is valuable information. Restate some of these reasons. If hypotheses are not supported, you must think creatively and speculate about practical and theoretical implications. This part of the discussion should focus on the relevance to theory for knowledge building and theory for practice.

Refer to Exercise 8 at the end of the chapter

As a social worker, extrapolating from your study to the intervention implications of your results is very important. Social work research is most often practice-oriented. Social workers want to know how to improve the planning and delivery of services to achieve desired and avoid undesired results. For example, social workers want to know whether your results point to a more precise assessment protocol they could use, how they might reinterpret presenting problems, or what specialized services need to be developed for a particular population.

Thus, a specific type of implication can point to a practical application. For example, the significance of the work is that it provides clear guidelines for how administrators and policy makers in hospice settings should communicate policy changes to frontline caregivers. But not all research has immediate practical applications, so if nothing practical comes to mind, do not force the point.

A relatively easy and concrete item for discussion is the practical application of the finding. Do this if it seems reasonable for the type of study under discussion.

Refer to Exercise 9 at the end of the chapter

Limitations and Directions
for Future Research

You should include a discussion of weaknesses of your study, but this should not be a big part of any Discussion section. After all, if the study were truly weak, you would not have undertaken to write about it. You are far more likely to discuss limitations rather than weaknesses. You should imagine yourself trying to out-fox potential critics of your study by acknowledging these shortcomings yourself. This concession has the effect of making the reader feel intelligent for having noticed something before you even mentioned it, rather than feeling argumentative about your conclusions.

Are the results generalizable to only a portion of the people to whom this hypothesis is supposed to apply? Of course. Indicate exactly what the limits of generalizability are. It is always possible to question the degree to which research results generalize outside the situation, but is there anything about yours that points especially strongly in that direction? Have you used correlational results to indicate the possibility of causality? Now is the time to remind the reader that this type of conclusion must be made with caution. Is it possible that someone else might have operationalized a construct in a different way than you did? Then admit it. However, feel free to defend your decisions in the same paragraph.

You are obligated to note the limitations of your study, but leave out the trivial ones and the ones that might apply to any study ever undertaken.

Refer to Exercises 10 and 11 at the end of the chapter

The last part of a Discussion section is often devoted to suggesting future research. Remember that this kind of suggestion must come directly from the discussion that precedes it. The limitations themselves often suggest how an improved study might be useful in the future.

Sometimes new writers, feeling the need to suggest some future research, propose something completely arbitrary. Be careful about this. For example, following a discussion of results related to color coding of baby food jars for new mothers who cannot read, it is not appropriate to suggest that future research be done on color-blind people or people who speak other languages. A sure sign that you are falling into the trap of suggesting irrelevant future research is a sentence that begins "It would be interesting to see if . . ." Suggest future research only if you can suggest what the next *logical* research question would be. And don't forget the verb lessons you have learned: If "future research" is to be the grammatical subject of the sentence, your verb choices are limited.

Refer to Exercise 12 at the end of the chapter

 **Exercise 1**

List subject-verb phrases found in the present tense in Discussion sections.

1. One explanation that may account for the results is that children who bully are exposed to various forms of victimization in their homes.

2. When both elderly adults are present, caregiver stress in adult children is sometimes mitigated.

3. Although these studies demonstrate that social work students have lower anxiety scores regarding research and statistics following a 2-week orientation, additional questions await further research.

4. _____
   _____
   _____

5. _____
   _____
   _____

6. _____
   _____
   _____

Exercise 2

List subject-verb phrases found in the past tense in Discussion sections.

1. The results of Study 3 showed that the presence of pets increased interaction among residents.

2. The present study examined the influence of culture and traditions on third-generation Aboriginal adults receiving government aid.

3. It is unlikely that our results were due to lack of teacher participation.

4. _____

_____

_____

5. _____

_____

_____

6. _____

_____

_____

Exercise 3

Select several Discussion sections and look at the first sentence or two of each. Copy examples of opening passages that state whether the main hypothesis was supported. When several hypotheses have been tested and several statistics have been reported, you may find that the author indicates which specific result or analysis is tied to a specific hypothesis. However, the Discussion section is not a place to *restate* the results but a place to explain and interpret them.

1. As expected, participants provided with an information kit prior to applying for social assistance completed their application and interview process more successfully than those provided with a first-aid kit.

2. The study reported here provides strong support for the general contention that intermittent reinforcement of temper tantrums increases their frequency and duration.

3. The present findings fail to support the hypothesis that female sole-parents parent more effectively than male sole-parents.

4. _____

_____

_____

_____

5. _____

_____

_____

_____

6. _____

_____

_____

_____

Exercise 4

Look for statements of similarity between this work and that of previous researchers or other works by the same author.

1. Our results support Hudson's (1997) findings that self-esteem and depression are inversely correlated.

2. _____

_____

_____

3. _____

_____

_____

 **Exercise 5**

Look for statements that show differences between this work and that of previous researchers.

1. Given the data from our study, it is clear that the problem of violence recidivism is not solved by completing an anger management course, as proposed by Harris (1993).

2. _____
    _____
    _____
    _____

3. _____
    _____
    _____
    _____

Exercise 6

Look for acknowledgment of alternative explanations for the findings—explanations other than the "truth" of the hypotheses or theories that appear to be supported.

1. Another possible cause for the higher dropout rates among participants in the parenting classes could be the outbreak of viral infections in the winter season.

2. _____
    _____
    _____
    _____

3. _____

_____

_____

_____

4. _____

_____

_____

_____

Exercise 7

Copy a few references to and explanations of negative results.

1. This assessment tool did not reliably distinguish first-year social work students from first-year psychology students on interviewing skills. It is possible that, contrary to our hypothesis, the selection of these majors is not dependent upon the level of interview skills already attained. Alternately, it may be that these majors are more likely to attract people-oriented students than other majors.

2. _____

_____

_____

_____

_____

3. _____

_____

_____

_____

_____

_____

4. _____

_____

_____

_____

_____

_____

Exercise 8

Look for comments that refer to theories or theoretical contexts
previously mentioned in the introduction.

1. These findings suggest a limit to the use of empowerment theory
in explaining the complex array of symptoms exhibited by
women who have been abused.

2. _____

_____

_____

_____

3. _____

_____

_____

_____

4. _____

_____

_____

_____

Exercise 9

List examples of how practical applications are mentioned in Discussion sections.

1. Social work educators and practitioners should be careful about . . .

2. These multiagency teams need to align more closely with case management functions in order to determine that a less restrictive placement for a child has been attempted.

3. Complexity of student learning styles such as that suggested by the significant interaction effects in this study should be included in courses of ethical concerns in social work.

4. _____

    _____

    _____

    _____

5. _____

    _____

    _____

Exercise 10

Look through Discussion sections for indications of the limitations of studies. List the types of limitations that you find.

1. The cross-sectional design does not give direct evidence of change in the variable of interest.

2. The findings are not generalizable to . . .

3. The self-report method provides only an indication of how people actually behave in the situation. . . .

4. _____

_____

_____

5. _____

_____

_____

6. _____

_____

_____

Exercise 11

List specific words and phrases that are used to present limitations.

1. One limitation of the study is that Hispanic executive directors may have responded in socially desirable ways.

2. One factor affecting the degree to which the study results can be generalized to other settings and populations is the specificity of variables.

3. We did not control for children's differing problem histories and maturation levels.

4. Three factors threaten the internal validity of this one-group pretest-posttest research design: differential participation period, limitations in recall, and instrumentation error.

5. _____

_____

6. _____

_____

7. _____

_____

8. _____

_____

Exercise 12

Copy phrases from suggestions for future research that indicate how the suggestions are tied to the rest of the discussion.

1. As suggested in the current study, future research should focus on identifying the specific needs of older women who have been abused.

2. Continued exploration . . . is necessary to determine which of the competing explanations might account for these findings in other school settings.

3. A study is needed that traces the increases in self-esteem in male batterers who have learning disabilities by comparing two groups over time.

4. _____

_____

_____

_____

5. _____

_____

_____

_____

6. _____

_____

_____

_____

9
Writing the Abstract

An abstract is a summary. It appears on a separate page following the title page. It is the part of the manuscript that the *reader* pursues first but that the *writer* approaches last. An abstract tells the reader the purpose of the study as well as the method, results, and conclusions. Abstracts reporting empirical studies are usually between 100 and 120 words. Abstracts for review or theoretical articles may be briefer. By the time you are ready to write your first abstract, you will already have read and used abstracts for at least some of the purposes for which they are intended. Understanding what readers need from your abstract is the best way to begin learning how to fulfill these needs. Readers you are addressing include the following:

1. *Someone who needs an overview of an article he or she is about to read.* This reader might be a student doing required reading, an expert determined to keep up with everything written in a certain narrow field, or someone who was so attracted by the title that nothing will stop the process. This type of reader needs an outline that will facilitate cognitive processing of the article. Technical writing is not dependent on surprise endings, and technical reading is aided when outcomes are known in advance.

2. *Someone who is browsing through a journal looking for something interesting.* This reader might be someone who

subscribes to the journal (probably an expert) or someone passing time in a library (perhaps an expert in a related field or a student). This reader appreciates that all abstracts follow a similar format so that quick comparisons of content can be made. This person wants to know how a certain article will advance his or her professional knowledge. Will it be relevant because of its theoretical context, methodology, or outcomes?

3. *Someone who is searching an abstract-retrieval system (such as Social Work Abstracts Plus, Psychological Abstracts, Sociological Abstracts, Current Contents, Sociofile, and so on).* It is impossible to imagine every purpose served by these databases, but consider just a few. Students use them to look for sources for a paper; professors look for relevant readings to assign; authors use them to determine which journals are most likely to publish articles like the one they are preparing; researchers look for data on a measure they are about to use; graduate school applicants look for articles written by the faculty of a program they are considering. Sometimes the outcome of these searches is a list of articles that the searcher intends to look at or read. At other times, it is a fact-checking mission and begins and ends with abstracts only. Yet other times, it is a fishing expedition, and the searcher must decide whether to examine entire articles.

How can all of these types of readers be served by the same 120-word summary? There are two parts to the answer. First, the contents are narrowly specified in the *Publication Manual*. Therefore, readers will always be able to predict that they will find certain types of facts in every abstract. Second, the style is designed so that it can stand alone and still be very informative.

An abstract contains 100 to 120 words.

Contents

The abstract of a research report should contain key facts from each section of the report. To accomplish this as the abstract writer, try using one sentence each from the Introduction, Results, and Discussion sections and up to two sentences from the Method section. This guideline should keep the new writer within the required word count while including the types of information specified in the *Publication Manual*.

From the introduction, extract the key element from the portion devoted to the purpose of the study and reduce it as much as you can. This information is usually contained in the first sentence of the abstract.

Refer to Exercise 1 at the end of the chapter

You must state facts about the participants that are particularly relevant to the study. Include at least number, age, and gender.

Refer to Exercise 2 at the end of the chapter

State the major elements of the method, including all procedures of the intervention and the names of measures. A well-known instrument may be included in the same sentence as the participant description. Alternatively, if the method is unusual, it is best to write two sentences—one about the measure used and one describing the participants.

Refer to Exercise 3 at the end of the chapter

State the major findings. Do this in English, not in statistics, but include significance levels. You will not have space for secondary findings. Indicate only those that refer to the major purpose expressed in the abstract.

Refer to Exercise 4 at the end of the chapter

Finally, the abstract contains a statement concerning the conclusions, implications, and/or applications of the study. Choose from the following types of statements: what was demonstrated, what the consequences are of what was demonstrated, or in what way the study should be appreciated and by whom.

Refer to Exercise 5 at the end of the chapter

Style

The best way to write your own abstract is to follow the guidelines above without concern for length in your first draft. When you have done that, you will probably find that you have gone over the 120-word limit. Before attending to some of the stylistic elements that will help shorten your abstract, go over it to make sure that it is accurate and self-contained. This editing session may even increase the length of your abstract, but consider why accuracy and completeness are so important. Many people, as described earlier, will never read your entire article. For their sake your abstract must be able to stand alone and to report reliably what is in the paper.

An abstract is accurate and self-contained. Some people will never read the rest of the article.

So reread your abstract, making sure that you have not included information that is not in your article and that you have included the major purpose, the result, and the contribution of your study. If you have extended or replicated someone else's work, reference to that work must also be in the abstract (authors' initials and surnames and year of publication). That way, someone following up the work of a certain author will find yours in a key-word search for that author. However, there is no references list associated with the abstract. The full reference information for studies referred to in your abstract will be found at the end of your paper in the regular references section.

Include the major purpose, the result, and the contribution of your study in the abstract.

The *Publication Manual* specifies that third person is preferable to first person in an abstract. It also instructs that verbs are preferable to their noun equivalents (e.g., *impair* rather than *impairment),* and that active voice is better than passive. Therefore, reread with an eye to how your sentences can be strengthened accordingly. For example, do not write "Participants were asked for their opinions about . . ." Change to more active language: "Participants rated . . ."

Use the active rather than passive voice in the abstract.

Now reread again, this time making sure that the abstract can stand alone. Do not use unusual abbreviations. Define terms that may not be known to a social worker with a different specialty. If you have given your treatment groups nicknames or acronyms, do not use them in the abstract (unless you will refer to them twice in the abstract; in that case, present acronyms in parentheses the first time, as you would in the paper itself).

Do not use unusual abbreviations in the abstract.

After you are sure you will not need to *add* anything else to your abstract, and assuming you are over the 120-word limit, it is time to see what characters, words, or phrases you can *delete*. First apply the rules that are specific to abstracts: Use numerals instead of words for numbers under 10, unless they begin a sentence; use abbreviations in the text that would normally be allowed only within parentheses (like *etc.* or *vs.*); use abbreviations or acronyms that are commonly understood by social workers even if you are using the terms only once (e.g., ANOVA and CBCL).

Use common abbreviations in the abstract without using whole words to introduce them.

Next look for phrases that are not dense with information and try to omit them. For example, omit "the results revealed that" and "the conclusions are that." Omit phrases that repeat information provided by the title of the paper.

See if sentences can be combined to save words. For example, perhaps you can include subject and method information in one sentence: "Undergraduate students (25 men and 25 women) rated 5 types of practicum exercises." You might be able to combine purpose and results by reordering and combining: "The hypothesis that concrete learners prefer nonwriting course assignments was supported in a study that assessed the preferred learning styles of undergraduate social work students."

Do not be discouraged if you are still over the limit. Writing an abstract is a very difficult task. Deleting words and phrases that have been written with great effort is an emotional and intellectual strain. Consider trading abstracts with another student if you still cannot find a place to delete words. It is often easier to delete phrases from someone else's work than your own.

When you finally feel that your abstract fulfills all the criteria discussed so far, you have only one task left. Imagine all the people who might search an abstract-retrieval database and be glad to find your abstract. What key words would these various people be likely to use in their search? Make sure that all those words are actually in your abstract so that all these potential searchers will find your work.

Include all the words that someone doing a key-word search would be likely to use.

In typing your abstract, note that it should be a single nonindented paragraph, double-spaced like the rest of the document. The word Abstract is capitalized and centered at the top of the page, just like other section headings.

Do not indent the first line.

Exercise 1

Copy the first sentence from abstracts that begin with a global statement of purpose.

1. Aims were to determine whether risk factors for maltreatment in the first year of life persisted into the second and third year of life.

2. This article constructs an integrated conceptual framework for understanding community violence based on a content analysis of different theories.

3. Attributions of blame for the first and latest episodes of violence were assessed in a sample of 139 couples who were referred to a mandatory domestic violence treatment program in the southern counties.

4. _____
    _____
    _____

5. _____
    _____
    _____

6. _____
    _____
    _____

Exercise 2

Copy statements from abstracts that provide facts about subjects or participants.

1. Fifty-seven men (86%) from a residence for seniors (aged 65–75) had social functioning impairment during the first year of living in the placement.

2. One hundred women and their mothers who were living in multigenerational households that included a child under age 5 were likely to report depressive symptoms to their physicians and were likely to have problems in caring for their children.

3. _____

_____

_____

_____

4. _____

_____

_____

_____

5. _____

_____

_____

_____

Exercise 3

Copy statements from an abstract that provide facts about methods.

1. Ninety-three 8- to 13-year-old children were asked moral reasoning questions based on an animal fable involving a moral dilemma. A key requisite for such studies is a valid and reliable scale for measuring moral reasoning, an example of which is described in this article.

2. The study group was composed of 296 individuals with a history of state psychiatric hospitalization. One group ($n = 188$) was currently receiving case management services; the control group ($n = 108$) was eligible for but not receiving case management services. Survival analysis models were tested to derive a model that contained the maximum number of significant variables for community living until rehospitalization.

3. _____

_____

_____

_____

_____

_____

4. _____

_____

_____

_____

_____

_____

Exercise 4

Copy statements of research findings from Abstracts.

1. Child neglect was associated with more negative views of self as a parent and high scores on the parenting potential scale ($p < .05$).

2. Eighty-eight percent of first-time adjudicated youth receiving 6 months of intense one-on-one prosocial adult supervision and living in family treatment settings did not reoffend in the 36 months following their return home.

3. _____

_____

_____

_____

4. _____

_____

_____

_____

 **Exercise 5**

Look at the final sentences of some abstracts. Copy statements or sentence frames that seem to summarize the major points of the Discussion sections.

1. In addition to the better-known measure of service assessment and service use, the family service potential inventory used in this study is an important predictor of family strengths assessment.

2. The findings indicate that child neglect may be a risk factor for more negative views of self as a parent, beyond differences between neglect and non-neglect samples in more general assessments of family-of-origin quality.

3. Findings extended prior research by demonstrating that . . .

4. _____
   _____
   _____
   _____

5. _____
   _____
   _____
   _____

6. _____
   _____
   _____
   _____

10
Listing References

Students often notice that APA style calls for a References section rather than a Bibliography. The difference is important. In your References section, you list the works you have *referred to* in your paper. A bibliography is usually more extensive than a references list and may contain material you read but did not cite. Your references list should be in one-to-one correspondence with the authors you have mentioned in your paper. It should be accurate; readers may wish to consult some of your sources for their own edification. It should not contain anything you did not actually have in front of your eyes; secondary sources should be listed when appropriate, rather than primary sources which you did not read.

Include in the references section only those sources that you cited in your paper and only those you actually consulted.

If you read only one chapter of a book, you must list only that chapter. Usually, this occurs in the case of an edited book with chapters by various authors. Sometimes, however, you will consult part of a book written by a single author. In this case, the *Publication Manual* provides specific formats for indicating which chapter and/or pages you consulted. There are so many types of material that may be consulted that it is not necessary to familiarize yourself with how to cite all of them until you need them. In this chapter, you will learn about the three most common types of references that occur in student papers: journal articles, chapters in edited books, and authored books (i.e., the same person[s] wrote the whole book). For all other types of references, please consult the *Publication Manual* for details.

Word Processing Tips

■ The references section begins on a new page, but it has a heading whose level is equivalent to the other major sections (e.g., Results), so it is typed, centered, at the top of the page. The rest of the manuscript (with the exception of the Abstract) is continuous; that is, no other section begins at the top of a page unless it happens to fall that way.

■ Double space everything on these pages, both within and between references on the list. Each entry should begin with a *hanging indent*. That means the first word is at the left margin and all other lines for that reference are indented ½ inch.

■ Never type authors' first or middle names. Use only their initials and leave a space between initials.

Alphabetizing

Alphabetize according to the last name of the author who is listed first in each source. Remember: Use initials, not full given names. Keep the following items in mind:

■ Do not rearrange the order of authorship of any given article or chapter. If the article lists the authors as Smith, R. T., & Jones, A. L., do not list them as Jones, A. L., & Smith, R. T.

■ Works by the same author are listed by year of publication, with the earliest first.

■ If you have the same author listed first with different coauthors for different articles, arrange the entries alphabetically within the listing for that author according to the second author of each entry. List Smith, R. T, & Jones, A. L. before Smith, R. T., & Marks, B. J.

■ If an author appears as a single author of one source and the first coauthor of another, list the single-author source first, then the one with the coauthor (following the principle that "nothing" goes before "something"). List Smith, R. T before Smith, R. T., & Jones, A. L.

Refer to Exercise 1 at the end of the chapter

Journal Article Reference

Author(s). (Year). Article title. *Journal Title, volume #,* page numbers.

Example:

Rogers, M. (1989). My sweater has a zipper. *Children's Television Review, 12,* 120–122.

■ With two authors, use an ampersand and comma between them.

Rogers, M., & Kermit, F. (1984). Not all sweaters have zippers. *Children's Television Review, 14,* 12–30.

■ With three authors:

Rogers, M., McDonald, R., & Kermit, F. (1984). Not all creatures wear sweaters. *Children's Television Review, 17,* 124–130.

■ With more than 6 authors, name the first 6, then et al.

Rogers, M., McDonald, R., Kermit, F., Bird, B., Mouse, M., Brown, C., et al. (1984). And so on . . .

Here are the rules:

1. Author(s), last name followed by initial(s).
   ■ Use the ampersand (&) before the last author.
   ■ Place a comma between authors on the list.
   ■ Place the comma before the ampersand, even if there are only two authors on the list.

2. Year of publication.

   ■ Place the year in parentheses.

   ■ Place a period after the parentheses.

3. Title of the article.

   ■ Capitalize only the first word in the title and the first word after a colon, when applicable.

   ■ End the title with a period.

4. Title of the journal.

   ■ Capitalize each important word.

   ■ Italicize the title of the journal.

   ■ Follow this with a comma.

5. Volume number of the journal.

   ■ Italicize the volume number of the journal.

   ■ Follow it with a comma.

6. Issue number.

   ■ Almost never include this. Do so only if each issue of the year starts with page 1. Usually, scholarly journals begin each *year* with page 1 and each *issue* begins with the page that follows the last one in the previous issue.

   ■ If you should have to do this, place in parentheses after the volume number, with no space between: *45*(1).

   ■ Do not italicize it.

7. Page numbers.

   ■ Include the full range (e.g., use 125–127, rather than 125–7 or 125–27).

   ■ Do not italicize the page numbers.

   ■ Finish with a period.

Chapter in an Edited Book

Chapter Author(s). (Year). Chapter title. In Book Author(s) (Ed[s].), *Book title* (page numbers of chapter). Place of Publication: Publishing Company.

Example:

> Smith, T. J., & Jones, R. N. (1971). Very interesting stuff: Relationship between grades and dental cavities. In J. Lennon & P. McCartney (Eds.), *A big book of interesting stuff* (pp. 22–125). London. British Publishing Co.

Here are the rules:

1. Chapter author(s)' last name(s) followed by a comma then by initial(s).

   ■ Same rules as for a journal article, above.

2. Year of publication.

   ■ Same rules as for a journal article, above.

3. Title of the chapter.

   ■ Same rules as for a journal article title, above.

4. The word "In" (not italicized).

5. Editor(s)' name(s).

   ■ Initial(s) then last name—not last name first.

   ■ Separated by commas and ampersand as for authors, but use no comma for only 2 authors.

6. (Ed.) or (Eds.).

   ■ Follow with a comma.

7. Title of the book.

   ■ Italicize the title.

   ■ Capitalize only the first word in the title and the first word after a colon, when applicable.

8. Page numbers of chapter.

   ■ Use the form pp. 10–32

   ■ Place in parentheses.

   ■ Follow with a period.

9. Place of publication.

   ■ Indicate city. Indicate state or country unless it is well–known. Separate City and state (country) with a comma.

   ■ Use postal abbreviations for state.

   ■ Follow with a colon.

10. Publishing company.

    ■ End with a period.

Refer to Exercise 2 at the end of the chapter

An Authored Book

This is a book written entirely by the same author(s) rather than with chapters contributed by various people. Our book is an example.

Author(s). (year). Title. City: Publisher.

Example:

Smart, I. M. (1995). *Fun with psychology.* Green Hill, IL: Green Publishing Co.

Refer to Exercise 3 at the end of the chapter

Electronic References

As with the material above, this section will not be an exhaustive guide to these formats. Consult the full document on the following Web site for formats not covered here: *http://www.apastyle.org/elecref.html*

When you want to cite an entire Web site, as we just did, do what we just did: give the address in the text and put no entry in the references list. But if there is a document you want to cite, notice that you can find all or most of the same elements you need for print documents. Include the author and date in the text and list the full citation on the references page. After you have included all the information specified for journal articles, indicate what date you retrieved it from the Web and the Web site. Here is an example for a journal article retrieved from the Web:

> Simpson, B. (1999). Cartooning and casework. *Journal of Multimedia Social Work, 2,* 220–227. Retrieved March 5, 2003, from *http://www.naswdc.org/simpson.html*

It is possible that the document you retrieve is not a journal article, but rather an item written by someone just for posting at the Web site. If that is the case, treat it more like a book when you list it. Here is an example:

> Simpson, B. (1999). *Cartooning and casework.* Hollywood, CA: National Association of Social Workers. Retrieved March 5, 2003 from *http://www.naswdc.org/simpson.html*

Be careful with final punctuation. Putting a period at the end of a sentence or reference entry that would come after the URL address can cause an error for someone searching for that site. If there is no period in the address itself, leave it off the sentence too. (See the last sentence in the first paragraph of this section.)

Capitalization rules for URLs are as follows: Everything up to and including the host name (*http://www.naswdc.org* in the example above) is in lower case. The rest must match exactly what you found on the Web.

Refer to Exercise 4 at the end of the chapter

References in the Body of the Manuscript

Citations in the text contain two parts: the author(s) and the year of publication. In the text your citation would look like this: "Szuchman and Thomlison (1991) validated the first measure of childhood suicide risk" or "As noted (Szuchman & Thomlison, 1991), the first measure of childhood suicide risk was validated" or "In 1991, Szuchman and Thomlison validated the first measure of childhood suicide risk."

When you are quoting from a source, use double quotation marks. Single quotation marks are used only when the author you are quoting is quoting someone else. In that case, the source contains double quotation marks, and these become single quotation marks in your manuscript. Final punctuation goes inside the quotation marks unless the quotation is followed by a page number in parentheses. When your quotation contains 40 or more words, use block form. That means that instead of using quotation marks, place the entire quotation in indented form. Indent 1/2 inch from the left margin (in line with the start of paragraphs) and keep every line of the quotation indented just the same amount. Do not change the right margin; use the same right margin as the rest of your manuscript.

You will have to cite the page number of the source for direct quotations. Do so after the closing quotation mark and before the period:

Thomlison and Szuchman (1990) reported "Blah blah blah" (p. 23).

If you want the authors' names in parentheses, do it like this:

"Blah blah blah" (Thomlison & Szuchman, 1990, p. 23).

When this occurs after a block quote it comes in after the final punctuation:

Mary had a little lamb, whose fleece was white as snow. Everywhere that Mary went the lamb was sure to go. He followed her to school one day which was against the rule. The teacher was surprised to see a lamb at school. (p. 23)

Here are some final quirks of APA referencing rules:

- Use the ampersand in parentheses and the word *and* in the text.

- Use commas only for three or more authors.

- When the work has two authors, always use both names (Szuchman & Thomlison, 1991).

- When the reference has more than two and fewer than six authors, always list all authors in the first reference to that work (Rothery, Thyer, Thomlison, Hudson, & Corcoran, 1997). In future citations in the text, name only the first and use *et al.* instead of the rest of the names on the list (Rothery et al., 1997). When the work has six or more authors use *et al.* after the first author's name even in the first reference.

- If you are referring to more than one article inside the same parentheses, use a semicolon to separate the references. List them in the same order as they would appear in the References section. Here is an example: "This hypothesis has robust support (Szuchman, 1996; Thomlison & Wong, 1998; Turner et al., 1995)."

- With groups as authors, cite the group the first time: (National Institute of Health [NIH], 1997). It is understood that the abbreviation followed by the publication year is acceptable in further citations. For example: "The NIH (1997) studied substance abuse assessment profiles of Cuban adolescents."

Exercise 1

Copy from a list of references two listings by the same author for works published in different years.

_____

_____

_____

_____

_____

_____

Copy two listings in which publications by two or more authors are headed by the same author.

_____

_____

_____

_____

_____

Exercise 2

Copy one listing for a chapter in an edited book.

_____

_____

_____

  ## Exercise 3

Copy a listing for an authored book.

_____

_____

_____

 ## Exercise 4

Go to _http://www.naswdc.org_ and search for a document you like. Cite it below:

_____

_____

_____

11
Preparing the Title Page and Formatting Your Manuscript

Many people write with a working title in their minds but find that the finished product is actually an imperfect match for the title originally proposed. The title is very important, and careful thought should be given to preparing a succinct and, preferably, interesting title. Students working on course assignments often use the title of the course as listed in the syllabus for the paper or research report, but that is an inappropriate title for the paper. It is common for both professionals and students to compose the final title after the manuscript is written.

Like any title page, the title page of your APA-style manuscript contains the title of your paper, your name, and other identifying data. In addition, it contains information unique to APA style that is intended for the convenience of the editor and the printer of the journal to which the article may be submitted: the manuscript page heading and the running head. The difficulties students have involve (a) composing a good title and (b) understanding the difference between the manuscript page heading and the running head.

Writing a Title

The *Publication Manual* directs that titles

- Be 10 to 12 words in length.

- Make sense standing alone.

■ Name the important variables or theoretical issues.

■ Identify the relationships among variables.

It is no wonder that students need practice in writing titles that conform to all these requirements. Often after accounting for variables and being sure to make sense, authors find themselves with very long first-try titles. That is nevertheless a good way to begin.

Write everything you think you need without worrying about length. At this point it helps to think of the problem as a word puzzle, and very often word puzzles can be fun. First, get rid of anything unnecessary, such as "A Study of" or "An Investigation of." The title "An Investigation of the Relationship Between Hat Sizes and Performance in Undergraduate Research Methods Classes" would benefit from that kind of cleanup.

Now you might find yourself with a title that starts with the words "The Relationship Between" or "The Effect of." Even though this is acceptable according to the *Publication Manual,* it is not the best way to start. First, it is likely that you can save words if you find another way to convey this idea. Second, it is wise to begin with a word of specific importance to your study, because when researchers glance through a list of titles in order to decide what to read, their attention is captured best by the first word. Can you phrase the title in the form of a question? This is often a good alternative: "Do Undergraduate and Graduate Social Work Students Wear Special Styles of Hats?" Choose your first word or phrase so that it applies uniquely to your own study. Some examples are "Child and Family Characteristics Associated with Outcomes in Foster Care"; "Social Security Reduction Effects on Older Adults"; "Development of an Instrument to Measure Restrictiveness"; and "A Controlled Evaluation of Service to Reduce Teen Pregnancy." Create titles that begin with important variables.

Refer to Exercise 1 at the end of the chapter

In scanning titles for the exercise above, you undoubtedly noticed many that began with "The Effect of." You have also seen some alternatives, and three probably stand out: the question title, the colon title, and the "and" title. The question title ("Does Violence Beget Violence?") works because it is attention grabbing. The colon title works because it allows important variables (gender and ethnicity) to be identified before the words *effect* or *relationship* are used (but these words can still be used for clarity). The "and" title names the variables, uses "and" between them, and depends on the reader to infer which is the dependent and which is the independent variable. If you use an "and" title, be sure there is little likelihood that a reader could make the wrong inference. In this case "Gender and Racial Discrimination Behaviors" is just as informative as "Racial Discrimination Behaviors and Gender."

Elements of the Title Page

Now that your title is written, you have only to follow some rules about getting it on a title page.

1. Type the title centered on the page. Capitalize important words. Do not capitalize every letter. Do not use a font different from what is in the body of the paper and do not use bold type. If you use two lines because your title cannot fit on one line, double-space between them and break the title at a meaningful point, not whenever the line is full.

2. Center your name one double space below the title. Decide today what your professional name will be. Most people use a first name and middle initial. Of course, some people have names that are more complex than others, with two middle names or a hyphenated last name. Decide how it should look, but do not stray far from the first name–middle initial–last name approach. Your name may change between your first publication and your last, but you should not change your professional name if you want people to know who you are. Again, use uppercase and lowercase letters, nothing fancy. Do not use the word *by*.

3. Center the name of your institution one double space below your name.

4. Your instructor may want additional information, such as course number and date. If you have no specific instructions, just stop with name and institutional affiliation.

5. Create a manuscript page header. Use the "header" command on your word processor to create a flush right header that starts with the title page. The header contains the first two or three words of the title (even if they make

no sense by themselves) followed by five spaces and then a page number. The reason for putting the beginning of the title in the header is that pages might be separated during the review and printing phases of journal work. Something handy must be used to identify which page goes with which manuscript (another good reason to avoid "effect of" titles). Your name is not appropriate because journal editors decide what to publish after articles are reviewed by people who do not see the name of the author.

6. Decide on a running head of 50 characters (letters, spaces, and punctuation all count). The running head is a short version of your title that *does* make sense. If your title itself contains fewer than 50 characters, use the whole title. The running head is what would be used as the page header in the actual printed journal and what readers use to find their place or remember what they are reading.

   ■ Place the running head on the title page flush left near the top.

   ■ Type the words *Running head* followed by a colon. Then type your running head in all uppercase letters. Here is an example: "Running head: PRACTICE VARIABLES."

Pay attention to the difference between the manuscript header and the running head. The manuscript header is on the top right of every page, contains the first 2 or 3 words of the title (often does not make sense) and the page number. The running head contains 50 characters or fewer, makes sense, and summarizes your title. It appears only on the title page, on the upper left.

Refer to Exercise 2 at the end of the chapter

Formatting

By the time you prepare your title page, you are probably just about finished with your paper. Read instructions in the *Publication Man-*

ual about the word processing of your manuscript. Here are a few things students sometimes forget.

1. The header should appear on the title page and all pages except figures. For figures, hand write the header on the back.

2. The running head appears only on the title page.

3. Start a new page after the abstract and for the references. Do not start any other sections with a new page.

4. Double-space everything. There are no exceptions.

5. Use a 12-point font that is easy to read and looks like standard printing or typing. Courier and Times New Roman are good choices.

6. Use at least a 1-inch margin on all sides. Your word processor's default setting should work fine for this.

7. All text is flush left. Do not allow your word processor to right- or full-justify your lines. The right margin should be "ragged." Look for an "alignment" command and choose "left."

8. Do not allow your word processor to hyphenate at the ends of lines. This will probably mean changing the default settings. Try locating "line and page breaks" somewhere in the paragraph or document menu. Any hyphen that appears at the end of the line should be a hard hyphen, which is a hyphen that is part of the correct spelling of the word.

9. Use your spell checker cautiously. It can help you spell words correctly if the combination of letters you have typed does not exist as a word. It will not help you if you type *there* instead of *their*. Use your spell checker, but after that, check again using your brain.

Word Processing: Do not begin the Method, Results, or Discussion sections on a new page. Double-space throughout. The right margin should be ragged. Do not end a line with a hyphen except when a hyphen is required as part of the spelling of that word.

 **Exercise 1**

It is worthwhile to look at some creative approaches to this "effect of" problem and work backward. Copy some titles that start with key words, and indicate how they would be written if the author had written a lazy "effect of" title instead:

1. Sometimes authors start with a catchy research question and then move on to the variables. "Does Violence Beget Violence? The Relationship Between Adolescents' Violent Behaviors and Parental Disciplinary Practices." This is better than "The effect of Parental Disciplinary Practices on Adolescents' Violent Behaviors."

2. Sometimes authors put variables up front. "Gender and Ethnicity: Effects on Service Utilization."

3. "Gender and Racial Discrimination Behaviors." This works better than "Effect of Gender on Racial Discrimination Behaviors."

4. _____
_____
_____

5. _____
_____
_____

6. _____
_____
_____

Exercise 2

Copy some running heads (look in the upper margins of journal articles) and the titles of the articles to which they refer.

1. Running head: GRANDPARENTS REARING GRANDCHILDREN
   Title: Evaluating the Effectiveness of Biological Support Services to Grandparents Rearing Grandchildren.

2. _____

   _____

   _____

3. _____

   _____

   _____

4. _____

   _____

   _____

12
Grammar and Punctuation Matters

Now you have a completed manuscript. Prepare to polish your paper with at least one more round of revision. After all, you want to make a good impression. You have put a lot of hard work into researching your topic. Do not spoil the impression it will make by failing to correct common grammar and punctuation mistakes and improve the flow.

Some people have a flair for rules of grammar and punctuation. They seem to be born knowing how to avoid run-on sentences. Others need to spend time learning these things, and some of these people get to college with a few gaps in their understanding. This chapter contains a review of some rules of punctuation and grammar to which most university students have already been exposed. We are reviewing only a few rules because a social work class is not the place to learn everything there is to know about grammar and punctuation. We have selected these particular rules because social work papers seem to call for them quite often, and, in our experience, social work professors complain that many papers they grade contain errors based on the failure to apply these rules. For each of these rules, we have provided at least one example of proper usage in social work journals. You find others.

Parallel Construction

Whenever elements of a sentence have the same function, their form has to be parallel. This simple rule must not be so simple because so many students just can't seem to get it right. Let's break it down.

Items in a Series

"The participants were women, over 21, and had red hair." The items in this series should be all nouns, all adjectival phrases, or all verb phrases, not a combination. Here are improved versions: *They were red-headed women over age 21.* (no longer a series) *They were female, aged 21 or over, and red-headed.* (a series of adjectives).

Refer to Exercise 1 at the end of the chapter

Verb Forms

Verb forms must be parallel when they are joined in a series or by any kind of connecting word. There is an error in this sentence: "Participants were left alone and were being watched through a two-way mirror." *Were left alone* is not parallel to *were being watched*. Correct it this way: "Participants were left alone and were watched . . ."

Here is another example: "Dogs are more influential than cats, thereby occupying more leadership positions." *Are* is the third person singular present tense form of the verb; it is not parallel to *-ing*. Correct it this way: "Dogs are more influential than cats, and so they occupy more leadership positions." *Occupy* is a third person singular present tense form.

This sentence also contains an error: "Participants were asked to read and they evaluated the stories." Both verbs should be passive or both should be active: "Participants were asked to read and evaluate the stories."

Refer to Exercise 2 at the end of the chapter

Half-Empty Comparisons

More likely than what? Older than whom?

The following rule will keep you from writing sentences that can be ambiguous: If you are using the comparative form of an adjective (the *-er* form, like older, faster, and better), be sure that the reader knows which two items are being compared. In conversation, this is usually not a problem. If you say, "It is more likely to rain today," your listener knows whether you mean more likely than to snow or more likely than tomorrow. When writing, however, it is sometimes hard to remember that your reader is not as well informed about your context or your motives as your listener might be in conversation. So when you write that the experimental group performed better on the posttest, for example, your reader does not know if you mean better on the posttest than on the pretest or better than the control group performed on the posttest. It is perfectly acceptable to write, "The experimental group performed better on the posttest than the control group did," or "The experimental group performed better on the posttest than on the pretest." On one of your drafts, read through looking only for comparatives and making sure they are unambiguous.

Another potential problem with comparisons is the failure to make the second part completely clear. Such a violation results in a sentence like this: "Participants rated the soda in the paper cups higher than the plastic." Did they like the soda better than the plastic?

Refer to Exercise 3 at the end of the chapter

Agreement Between Subject and Verb

Subject-verb agreement is typically a problem only when a lot of words intervene between subject and verb. When that happens, many writers allow the verb to agree in number with whatever noun is nearby, even though that noun is not the grammatical subject of the sentence. Here are some long sentences in which subject and verb agree:

- The *goal* of all but a few (and those few were the only naturalistic experiments ever conducted on communication between humans and mole rats) of Smith's studies *was* unfathomable.

- The *objectives* of the present study, albeit obscure and perhaps not amenable to unbiased interpretation by all but a few highly educated social work students, as was also common in the research of Casteneda, *were* altruistic.

- The unrealistic *nature* of the participants' responses to the frightening scenarios *was* surprising.

Agreement Between Noun and Pronoun

Students come to college knowing that pronouns must agree in number with the nouns to which they refer. However, in writing social work papers, students often fail to achieve perfect agreement between nouns and pronouns. The problem is most frequent with the possessive *their.* One cause is the effort to use the nonsexist phrase *he or she* as the subject of the sentence, then later referring to, for example, *their* left hand. Remember that *each* is singular (each person *cannot* use *their* pencil). This type of error is so common that you should give your paper a read-through just to check every *their* against its referent. The best solution is usually to choose a plural form for the sentence's subject, then use all the plural pronouns you want afterward.

The problem also arises in the following construction: "When a child becomes aggressive, they often need a nap." The author of this sentence has mixed up *a child* and *they.* Here are some ways out: "A nap often helps when a child has become aggressive." "When a child becomes aggressive, put that child to sleep for a nap." "When children become aggressive, they often need naps."

Refer to Exercise 4 at the end of the chapter

Run-on Sentence or Comma Splice

To understand once and for all how to avoid run-on sentences, you will have to back up and understand once and for all what an independent clause is. A *clause* is a group of related words containing a subject and a verb. An *independent clause* makes complete sense and can be a stand-alone sentence. A *dependent clause* also contains a subject and a verb, but cannot stand alone—it begins with a word that ruins the whole prospect of its looking like a sentence. It does not make sense alone, because that little introductory word makes the whole clause *dependent* on another part of the sentence to make sense.

- ■ Independent clause: The participants ate the sausages.

- ■ Dependent clause: Although the participants ate the sausages . . .

You may not join two independent clauses with a comma. (If you do, you have written a run-on sentence, or a comma splice.) For example: The participants ate the sausages, the experimenter watched. (run-on sentence)

To correct the situation you have three choices: (a) Make two sentences by trading the comma for a period; (b) trade the comma for a semicolon—after all, something made you think these two sentences felt like one; or (c) join the two with a *coordinating conjunction*. Memorize the list of coordinating conjunctions now:

and   but   for   nor   or   so   yet   whereas

Getting back to the original problem, here are some solutions:

The participants ate the sausages; the experimenter watched.

The participants ate the sausages. The experimenter watched.

The participants ate the sausages, and the experimenter watched.

Refer to Exercise 5 at the end of the chapter

The other way to get into trouble with a run-on sentence is to join two independent clauses with the wrong kind of conjunctive word: a *conjunctive adverb*. Here is an example: "The participants ate the sausages, however, the experimenters never saw a thing." *However* is one of the words (conjunctive adverbs) that cannot join two independent clauses. When you find one of these run-ons in your work, make two sentences out of it: "The participants ate the sausages. However, the experimenters never saw a thing."

Here is a list of conjunctive adverbs that are likely to get you into this type of trouble:

afterward	likewise
also	moreover
besides	nevertheless
consequently	otherwise
furthermore	similarly
however	then
indeed	therefore
later	thus

Notice what lovely words they are when they begin sentences. Use them whenever you can. Just don't use them to join two independent clauses.

Colons with Lists

Sometimes a colon introduces a list. Some students use a colon to introduce every list. However, if you have a word or phrase that indicates the list is on its way, use a comma instead. These are some common examples:

for example   for instance   namely   that is

An exception to this rule is *as follows* or *the following*. These list-introducing phrases *do* take a colon. Another exception is *such as*. That one has *no* punctuation before the list. Sometimes a list just serves as the object of a verb: "The participants touched turtles, snakes, lizards, and jellyfish." If you would normally put a colon after the word *touched* in that sentence, stop it.

If it sounds to you as if most lists need no colons, you're about right. The only really good reason to use a colon (other than *as follows* and *the following*) is when an entire sentence (or independent clause) introduces the list, as in the examples in Exercise 6.

Refer to Exercise 6 at the end of the chapter

Comma Before *and* (and Sometimes *or*)

Some students use an incorrect rule that looks like this: Use a comma before every *and* and, while you're at it, every *or*. This mistake is probably the result of overlearning this rule: Use a comma before the *and* (actually, before any of the coordinating conjunctions) that coordinates two independent clauses. It might also be the result of this one: Use a comma before the *and* (and *or*) that signals the last item in a series.

There is no comma allowed before the *and* in a compound subject or compound predicate (unless there is a series longer than two—if that is the case, use the series rule for commas). Here is an example of this error: "The participants read every fourth word, and ate every third olive." No comma is allowed in that sentence—take it out: "The participants read every fourth word and ate every third olive." That *and* simply joins the two parts of a compound predicate. Without the nonsense, it just says they read and ate. You would never insert a comma if that's all it said: "They read and ate."

The same goes for a compound subject: "The fourth-grade boys with shoes, and the third-grade girls with hats traded insults." That comma is unacceptable; take it out. It merely joins the two parts of a compound subject: "The boys and girls traded insults." When you think you need a comma before a coordinating conjunction, find the bare bones of the sentence and see how the comma feels. If still feels good, do it.

Refer to Exercise 7 at the end of the chapter

A Comma When You Need a Breath

It's easy to see why you might be tempted to use a comma when sentence parts get very long: You need a breath. However, needing a breath is an absolutely unacceptable use of the comma. If that is really the only reason you can think of, don't do it. Sometimes this mistake results in the placement of a comma between the subject and the predicate—something no one would do on purpose.

Refer to Exercise 8 at the end of the chapter

Important Differences
Between People and Things

The relative pronoun *who* is for people. You may never use anything else. This sentence contains a common mistake: "The participants *that* were in the first group rode horses." If participants are people, use *who* instead of *that*.

Refer to Exercise 9 at the end of the chapter

 **Exercise 1**

Find examples of parallelism in series. Underline the parallel words.

1. These included <u>eating</u> plums, <u>preparing</u> simple meals with plums, <u>researching</u> plums, <u>selling</u> plums, <u>buying</u> plums, and <u>growing</u> high-quality plums.

2. Low self-esteem is characterized by <u>depression</u> concerning bad hair, <u>obsession</u> with always being perfect in appearance, and <u>unwillingness</u> to engage in confrontations.

3. _____

    _____

    _____

4. _____

    _____

    _____

5. _____

    _____

    _____

Exercise 2

Find examples of parallel verb forms with conjunctions or with series.

1. Participants completed a questionnaire for the first 5 minutes, banged their feet on a wall for the next 5 minutes, and completed a second questionnaire in the final 5 minutes.

2. The clinical social workers were praised and were given cake by the dean.

3. _____
_____
_____
_____

4. _____
_____
_____
_____

Exercise 3

Find sentences containing comparisons.

1. Participants associated more positive emotions with the photographs of the house than with those of the dog.

2. _____
_____
_____

3. _____
_____
_____

Exercise 4

Find some sentences with pronouns. Underline the pronoun and the noun to which it refers.

1. We isolated <u>participants</u> by placing <u>them</u> in cardboard boxes.

2. Freud emphasized the <u>individual's</u> need for soft drinks as well as <u>his or her</u> confrontation with sexuality.

3. _____
_____
_____

4. _____

_____

_____

5. _____

_____

_____

Exercise 5

Find some examples of sentences with two independent clauses joined by a coordinating conjunction.

1. We instructed participants to sit comfortably, yet we provided no chairs.

2. These results show no relationship between gender and hair length, but they support the results of previous studies.

3. _____

_____

_____

4. _____

_____

_____

5. _____

_____

_____

Exercise 6

Find examples of colon usage with lists.

1. There were three conditions: turtle scenario, snake scenario, and lizard scenario.

2. The experimenter gave these instructions: Complete the questionnaire and draw a birthday cake on the back of each page.

3. _____

    _____

    _____

4. _____

    _____

    _____

5. _____

    _____

    _____

Exercise 7

Find sentences with wordy compound subjects, predicates, and objects. Notice that they do not have commas—unless the compound is of three or more items, of course.

1. This startling claim was supported by a statistical analysis that failed to find a significant direct relation between age and ability to dance the tango but that did find significant relationships between age and a positive view of tango dancers and between a positive view of tango dancers and the ability to tango.

2. This is assessed by a decrease in heart rate and/or an increase in vigilance in response to pushes and shoves as a consequence of prior exposure to pushes and shoves.

3. _____

_____

_____

_____

4. _____

_____

_____

_____

Exercise 8

Read the sentences from the previous exercise aloud. Even though they have no commas, feel free to take a breath while saying them.

Exercise 9

Find sentences with people referred to by the relative pronoun *who*.

1. Individuals who went to bed early were likely to wake up wealthier and wiser than those who went to bed late.

2. Participants who did not return for the second session were isolated and scolded.

3. _____

_____

4. _____

_____

5. _____

_____

13
Polishing the Paper

You are probably not surprised to learn that after writing the first draft of your paper, you still have work to do. But the worst is over, so give yourself a moment to enjoy that feeling. We have named this chapter "Polishing the Paper" because the phrase has two meanings. Think of the rewriting and editing you do after the first draft in two ways: (a) You will now finish up your project, and (b) you will do what is necessary to make it shine.

Students sometimes call this proofreading, but that is not the correct word. It makes it sound as if after your first draft all you have to do is check it over for typing and spelling errors. That is what you do with the last draft, which is a bit farther down the line. Polishing the paper comprises three steps: *First, you revise; second, you edit; third, you proofread.* Each of these steps may involve more than one draft.

Step 1: Rewrite and Revise

The first rewrite (resulting in the second draft) must be conceptual. This will be a long process, so save yourself a day to do it. The best approach is to finish your first draft two full days before it is due (assuming that you can devote a big part of those two days to this paper—otherwise, allow extra days). In this rewrite you will not give style a thought. You are revising the paper so that it is well organized and flows logically.

Introduction

Think through your sequencing of paragraphs. Try to remember what your purpose was for each one, and now review the order to see if it is correct. Check to make sure that you have included all the following pieces of your argument in the proper places:

- The purpose of your study

- Why it is important

- Hypotheses or research questions

- Rationales for hypotheses

- General information about method

- Definitions of variables

Look for paragraphs with only one or two sentences. If you find any, fix them now. Either elaborate on what you have written, move the material to a more logical place, or remove those sentences.

Now try to outline your introduction. Outline what is really there, not what you meant to write. Step back and see if that outline is the best possible organization of your material. If you see whole paragraphs in the wrong place, move them. After they have been moved, make sure the transitions still work. Change them if they don't. If you see gaps where something should be explained or fleshed out, do it.

Check your subheadings. See if they still work now that you have made some changes. Can you improve on them? If you have not used subheadings, consider putting some in now.

Method and Procedure

First, look over your subheadings and make sure they accurately describe the material in each section. Next, examine the information you provide about participants. Check to be sure you have reported the essentials:

- Age and gender

- Type of population participants represent (e.g., first-year social work students)

■ Compensation they received for participating

■ How many did not complete the study and why

■ Appropriate demographic information for each group (if applicable)

If you used a measure, check to be sure you

■ Provided enough information for replication

■ Made clear the experience participants had using it

■ Indicated how readers could obtain it

If you have a special section for description of measures, does it stand alone or depend on information about conditions? If it makes no sense to someone as yet unfamiliar with your conditions, reorganize now. If you have used materials created by you, such as a special log or journal book for the participants, check that you have included the appropriate information describing the process used to develop and establish the instrument for others to replicate. Be sure you have provided all the steps in the process. What was kept in the measure and what was deleted during the development process? Have you provided examples? Is there enough information to replicate?

Look at the procedure. Try very hard to put yourself in the shoes of someone who wasn't there. Are there any sentences that wouldn't make sense for that person? If so, they are not necessarily bad sentences; more likely, they are in the wrong place. The best thing would be to try this section out on a friend. As you read it aloud, watch that person's face. If you notice a funny look, you have skipped some information that your audience needs in order to put the pieces together clearly. Alternatively, have the friend read the section aloud to you.

Check to be sure you have

■ Done a good job conveying the instructions that you gave to participants

■ Provided enough information to replicate

■ Included instructions on scoring (if applicable)

Results

Look at your original data analysis. Make sure that every analysis that should be in your paper is there. Double check *every* number against the printout from the statistics package you used or against the calculation that you did. This is also a good time to make sure that letters used in reporting statistics (e.g., *t, n, F, p*) are italicized (but not the Greek letters).

If you have used tables or figures to display data, each of them should be mentioned in this section. There should be enough information in the text to allow the reader to know what types of data are in the tables and figures. Also, the relevant means and percentages should be either in the text or in tables (or figures), not in both places.

Discussion

With your introduction on one side and your discussion on the other, check that every hypothesis or question mentioned in one is mentioned in the other. Then do the same thing with your results on one side and your discussion on the other.

Now outline your Discussion section. If you have only topics and no subtopics in your outline, you may have restated your results without discussing them. Remember your options:

- Similarities between your findings and someone else's

- Differences between your findings and someone else's

- Relationship between these findings and theories mentioned in the introduction

- Alternative explanations for the findings

- Suggested explanations for negative results

- Limitations of the study

- Implications of the findings

- Practical applications

- Suggestions for further research (with rationales)

References

This is a good time to check your references. Every reference in your paper should be on your references list and vice versa. Check the spellings while you are at it; your spell checker won't pick up errors in people's names.

Abstract

The last part of the first rewrite is checking the abstract. Assuming that you worked hard to get it right the first time, at this point you only have to double-check to make sure that any changes you made in the body of the paper do not affect the abstract. If you are still pleased with it, move on to the next step of polishing your paper.

Step 2: Edit and Rewrite

With your major revisions behind you, it is time to concentrate on organization and style. You are probably tired of the paper by now, but that is to be expected. You will learn to love this paper again before you hand it in because it will be so polished.

Begin with the paragraphs. Does each one start with a topic sentence? Does something about that sentence make clear why the paragraph is located where it is? For example, is there a subheading nearby that makes the reader expect such a topic? Is there a transition word that relates to the previous paragraph? Remember, you have a list in chapter 3—use it. Finally, does every sentence in that paragraph relate to the topic? Now you have to check every sentence for gross errors. First, make sure each sentence is really a sentence—not a run-on or a fragment. Next, find the grammatical subject of every sentence and underline it. Then, make sure the verb is appropriate in number. While you are at it, make sure the verb defines an action that is logically possible for the subject. For example, if you have written that a study *tried* to do something, now is the time to reconsider. Think about misplaced modifiers at this time. Admittedly, misplaced modifiers are not easy to spot in your own work, but sometimes when you are studying your sentences this closely, you can spot them.

This is also the time to check for errors in parallel construction. These, too, can be hard to spot; look especially at items in a series, at compound verbs, and at phrases containing comparisons.

Step 3: Proofread (Not a Rewrite)

You are nearing the home stretch, preparing to put a shine on that paper. Pass your eyes over your paper again. Circle the commas and colons. Try to remind yourself of the actual rule you learned in school or in this book that prescribes that punctuation mark in that place. You should have a grammar book somewhere on your desk; perhaps you can find that rule. If you can't specify the rule, you should seriously consider omitting the punctuation mark. Most of what is left can be streamlined with the use of the search function on your word processor. If you are not yet familiar with this function, take some time now to figure out how to *find* or *search* for a word or phrase. Also, it is a good idea to figure out the command that takes you to the top of your document because it will be efficient to return there after each search.

When you are ready, search for and correct the following, if necessary:

- *Apostrophe:* For each one, if it is used in a contraction, change the contraction to a more formal phrase. If it is a simple plural with no possession intended, omit the apostrophe. If the intention is possessive, but the word is a pronoun, omit the apostrophe. If it is a possessive noun, note whether it is singular or plural and make sure the apostrophe is in the right place.

- *Their:* First, make sure you didn't mean to write *there*. When that is taken care of, check that the noun referred to is apparent to the reader and that it is plural. Then do a search for *there* just to make sure you didn't mean to write *their*.

- *Feel, felt, think, thought, believe, believed, say, said, state, stated, prove,* and *proved:* If these refer to the activities of researchers you have cited, think it over. Perhaps you should substitute one of the words from your list of researcher verbs in chapter 3.

- *Current* and *present:* Do not use these words to refer to studies other than yours.

- *Data, hypotheses, hypothesis, stimulus, stimuli, analysis, analyses, phenomena, phenomenon, criteria,* and *criterion:* There is always a danger that the verbs in these sentences might not agree in number with these nouns.

- *Since* and *while:* Remember, the *Publication Manual* specifies that these words are only used in their temporal sense. You may need to substitute *because* and *whereas* if they are more accurate.

- *Between* and *among:* Use between for two things, among for more than two.

- *You* and *we:* Unless you are quoting instructions to participants, rephrase without these words.

- *Non, pre, post,* and *sub:* These are not words. They have to be attached to other words.

- *&: Ampersands* should appear only in parentheses. Authors' names are joined by *and* outside parentheses.

- *Latin abbreviations:* Make sure that they are punctuated correctly and that they appear only in parentheses except when *et al.* is used in a citation (Smith et al., 1998).

Now you can run your spell checker. It won't help you with names, so look them over each time the spell checker finds them. Check the spelling yourself.

Final Touches

You have only one task left. Read your paper aloud. Read every word you have written. This is the way you will notice whether you have left little words out or put extra ones in. All writers have trouble seeing dumb little mistakes because we know what something is supposed to say. Cognitive psychologists call this "top-down" processing; our minds are working with meaning, so sometimes our eyes miss the details.

This is the time when you begin to feel proud of your work; you are not feeling as sick of it as you were by the second revision. This is because you can appreciate how many little improvements you made even after you thought you were finished. You can finally take this paper out in public (or hand it in to your professor), and it will surely make a good impression.

14
Preparing a Poster Presentation

Many students are required to prepare a report or a review paper in the form of a poster presentation for at least one social work class. Moreover, because your first professional presentation of your research is more likely to be in the form of a poster presentation, in either the research methods class or practice methods class it is helpful to learn the guidelines for constructing and presenting a poster paper. There are also several regional and national social work research conferences every year that feature poster presentations. Posters are a particularly interesting method of visually presenting information. Preparing a poster paper for a conference is a good way to participate in professional forums if you don't feel ready to do an oral paper.

What Is a Poster Session?

A poster paper is a visual presentation of information in a summarized format. Posters always include a presentation of data from a research study or topical review. Posters of research studies usually present data from a large body of data with careful attention to the presentation of the research design and data analysis. It is also an effective way to present the results from smaller studies, such as work with a child, a single-subject design study, small-group designs, or other intervention elements of special visual interest. Posters of topical reviews usually present the theoretical framework, the key concepts, the literature search method, and the synthesized and organized results of the review.

Research is presented in the form of a display covering a board measuring about 4 by 6 feet, either vertically or horizontally. People can walk by and read the information and often discuss the findings and project with the presenter. Posters are arranged in rows filling the room reserved for this purpose. The posters may fill a room as large as a convention hall or as small as a classroom. You, the researcher, stand in front of your display, and interested persons stop, read, chat, ask questions, and offer advice. This goes on for 1 to 2 hours. At some conferences, the posters will remain during the conference. At others, posters will change during the conference to enable many people to present.

Presenting a poster has advantages over presenting a talk. For one thing, it is less frightening. For another, only people who really have an interest in your work are paying attention, and you have their full attention. You may come away with ideas for improvement for the next study or ways in which the current data could be better presented. Observers can ask questions and spend as little or as much time with a presentation as they want. The disadvantage is that it requires some serious planning to make the presentation as reader friendly as possible in this type of situation. People will be on their feet, they will be distracted by a lot of ambient noise, and they will be unsure about how much time to commit to any given poster in light of what remains to be seen. Developing strong empathy for the consumer's plight will help you decide what to present on your poster and how to display it.

Even though poster presentations are increasingly popular as methods of dissemination of research findings, the *Publication Manual* provides no guidance in preparing one. What, then, do authors rely on for poster rules? First, when a poster is accepted for presentation, presenters are usually provided with very brief guidelines from the organization sponsoring the conference. These generally include

1. The size of the display area each author will have.

2. The suggestion that the poster should be readable from a distance of about 6 feet.

3. Suggestions for letter sizes (Taylor, 1998):

title of presentation	1½-inch letters
author	1-inch letters
affiliation and headings	1-inch letters
text	¼-inch letters

4. A diagram of possible arrangements of title, abstract, introduction, method, results, and conclusions.

The poster must be readable from a distance of 6 feet.

Although these are useful guidelines, the second method for learning how to present your findings in poster format is even more effective: Go to a poster session. You will see that there are limitless ways to follow the general rules provided by the conference organizers, and you may even see that some people have ignored some rules completely, but that other rules are generally followed. You will quickly learn, for example, that the rule about the font being legible from a distance is not a good one to break, because no one seems tempted to read the posters with small print. Students in or near major metropolitan areas may have the opportunity to attend a national or regional social work meeting that includes poster presentations. If your agency or professional association has an annual forum of some type, don't miss it.

You are not bound to APA style—only the spirit of the style. That means that you must be clear, fair to those whose work came before yours, and intellectually honest about the positive and negative sides of what you have done. But it also means that you do not need to follow a rigid format. You can use numbered lists or bulleted points instead of paragraphs, for example. You can use tables or circles and arrows to illustrate your theories or research design.

Posters are true to the spirit of APA format, but the rules of presentation are relaxed.

Components of the Poster

A poster will have more or less the same components of a research study. The required sections are the Title, Abstract, Method, and Results sections. Other information or headings may be considered.

Title and Authors

The title, author, and affiliations are the same as you would prepare for a research report. Center this information at the top on a separate page. Use the same abstract that you would prepare for a written research report on your topic. This is the only section that can remain unchanged.

Introduction

The introduction will have to be very different from the one you would prepare for a written report. You have to include the purpose and significance of your topic and your hypotheses, but you must reduce the literature review considerably. Here are some ways to highlight relevant literature.

1. Discuss the first study to address your topic in its current form. Then describe a very relevant recent one, especially if you are replicating and extending it. There may be more than one very similar to yours; mention several of the most similar.

2. Discuss the competing theoretical positions surrounding your work. Then describe the study that most resembles your method.

3. Provide a general explanation without references about how this problem has been traditionally addressed in research. Then explain, with references if appropriate, how you will diverge from this tradition and why.

Keep the introduction as short as you can. Try to keep it to two or three pages of large type. Remember the distractions that the reader faces. In these situations, people may only read a part of what you have written. If there is a crucial section of the introduction that you want to be viewers read, make it visually distinct from the rest. Do this with the tricks your computer can produce, such as bullets, frames, bold italics, and color.

Make the Introduction section no longer than three large-type pages.

Method

The Method section has the potential to attract the most attention. Here you briefly describe your research method and/or summarize the interventions. Decide what is the most efficient way for someone to get the feeling of what the participants experienced. You may want to post the materials themselves (or portions of them). If you showed pictures, post the pictures. If participants read vignettes, put up a sample. If they performed a task with a piece of equipment, include a snapshot of someone using the equipment. If they made copies of drawings, put up a sample of the drawing and a sample copy. You do not have to provide the detail necessary to replicate; you have to provide the minimum necessary for someone to understand what you did. Of course, if you borrowed any of the details from a previous author, you will need to provide the references. In a brief narrative of the method and procedures, include enough to satisfy the observer that you did it right:

- The number of participants and any important data about them

- The design

- A brief description of the procedures

- The grouping of variables

- The nature of the control condition, if used

- The instruments used to measure the variables

Consider posting parts or photos of the actual materials.

Results

The results you post will be primarily tables and figures. If possible, present the results in graphic form, rather than in a table. Bar charts, graphs, and pie charts communicate best. Include easy-to-read titles and labels. You need only introduce them with a statement of the analyses you conducted and the significant findings.

Conclusions

Instead of a Discussion section, posters usually have Conclusions. The difference is that conclusions are less speculative and more directly tied to the hypotheses and results. There is no room for implications or suggestions for future research. Conclusions can be a few numbered points that you make about the relationship between the results and the hypotheses or research questions.

Posters usually have Conclusions, presented in bulleted or numbered highlights, in place of a Discussion.

References

You will have to prepare the References section if you referred to others' work. Occasionally, you will see posters written without references, but students should plan on a brief list of references.

Preparing the Poster

After you have prepared a draft of your poster, try printing a page in a large font. Choose a font that is easy to read, such as Times Roman, Bookman, Courier, or Century Schoolbook. You should experiment with a few variations, and include some bold fonts. You may want to try a landscape (sideways) orientation and see how that looks. Ask a friend to stand 6 feet back from your samples and help you decide which is easiest to read. When you are satisfied, print it all and see how much space it actually fills. Lay it out in various ways, always keeping pieces of the same section close together and putting some extra space between sections. Decide whether your audience will be reading across or down, and keep it consistent. Be sure the sequence is easy for the reader to understand. Number your pages or use arrows to help the readers move through the material in the manner you deem appropriate. Be sure to use a 20-pound paper or heavier. You may even consider mounting your presentation on a backing material.

Make it easy for the reader to understand the sequence in which pages should be read.

If you find that you have completely filled a 4- by 6-foot space with paper, you have written too much. Don't make it too daunting for that poster session attendee who is just milling around looking for something interesting to read. If your poster has some empty space, it will have more appeal and be more likely to be read by more people than if it is a board completely filled with writing. Experimenting with large fonts should provide you with opportunities to see which area jumps out most clearly. It will be one of the tables, photos, diagrams, bulleted lists, or an otherwise distinct section. Be sure you are happy with what jumps out. If someone reads only one part, it will be that part. Will it be the right one? This is the time to be sure that you have made visually distinct the areas that you want to be read first.

Finally, you must prepare a title banner. The type for the title, author, and affiliation must be larger than that used in the body of the poster. You can experiment with placing a title section across the center of the top or the abstract page on the top left and the title banner to the right of it. You will probably spend a lot of time arranging and rearranging the pieces.

When you are satisfied that you have arranged just the right amount of material in the space allotted for your poster, you can think about adding the final touches of visual appeal: a piece of colored paper behind each of your sheets; section titles backed separately on colored paper; a band of color framing each page; all pages mounted on lightweight poster board; two colors versus one color framing each page. But remember that the goal of the presentation is attracting the attention of attendees at a scientific meeting who are looking for something easy on the eyes and interesting to read. Remember that you are showing off your scientist side more than your artist side at this event. Don't be tempted to spend more time on form than on substance.

Some people find it easier to use one large sheet of paper, for example 36″ × 48″. They use a program like PowerPoint and put all of the text and graphics on one slide. This can be printed on a printer that handles oversized paper. This printing service is available in copy shops like Kinko's, and the price for a black and white poster is very modest. Color printing in this format is expensive. But black and white looks fine.

Finally, reduce the contents of your poster back to a 10- or 12-point font and reproduce it for handouts. Conference organizers often suggest how many to prepare. If this is an in-house function, your instructor will guide you. People who browse posters expect to have a hard copy available to take home for future reference. Be sure to include your address and e-mail address on the title page. If you have used a slide presentation format for your poster, you can reduce it to normal size and use it as a handout. The print is very small, but people are accustomed to getting this type of handout.

Preparing Yourself

What will actually happen at the poster session is that strangers will walk up to your poster, give it a glance, and do one of three things:

1. Walk away

2. Read it

3. Talk to you

If it is the first, you feel rejected. No one can adequately prepare for that. If it is the second, you wonder what to do with yourself while this happens. Again, until it happens, you can't know how to prepare. You may ask if they would like to know more, or if they have any questions you can answer. But if it is the third, you can be prepared. That is because people always say approximately the same thing: "Tell me the quick version of what you did." You went to all the trouble of making it artistic, easy to read, self-standing. Yet this stranger wants you to tell it? Shocking! But you can be ready. Go for the visual space that you designed to stand out; point to it and give your already prepared quick oral version. If this is an in-house event such as a classroom poster presentation, you may feel less anxious. If this is a professional meeting for social workers, prepare for the audience.

Finally, here is advice from our own research methods classes. After the students presented posters for the first time, we asked for the single most important piece of advice that they would give to next year's class. Their answer? Eat lunch first and wear comfortable shoes!

Appendixes

The appendixes on the following pages provide examples of the written elements of a research study as discussed throughout this book.

Appendix A: Sample Research Report/Proposal Outline

Appendix B: Sample Theoretical/Concept Review Paper Outline

Appendix C: Sample Title Page for a Journal Manuscript

Appendix D: Sample Abstract Page

Appendix A

Sample Research Report/
Proposal Outline*

Title Page
Abstract Page
Text or Body of Paper
   Introduction (do not use as a heading)
      Research question(s)
      Significance and purpose of study
      Relevance to social work
   Literature Review
      Theories, concepts, variables
      Empirical studies
   Method (this may vary but can be divided as below)
      Participants or clients (characteristics of sample)
      Research design
      Procedure (e.g., intervention)
      Outcome measures (dependent variables measurement)
   †Results
      Descriptive presentation of findings
   †Discussion
      Interpretation of findings
      Limitations of the study
      Implications and recommendations for social work
References
†Tables
†Figures
Appendixes
   Consent form
   Research instruments

---

*Adapted from Thyer, B. A. (1994). *Successful publishing in scholarly journals*. Thousand Oaks, CA: Sage Publications.
†Do not include these items in a research proposal

Appendix B

Sample Theoretical/Concept Review Paper Outline

Title Page
Abstract Page
Text or Body of Paper
    Introduction (do not use as a heading)
        Problem, issues, topic of the review
        Significance and purpose of the review
        Scope, focus, and approach of the literature review
        Relevance to social work practice, research, or social policy
    Literature Review
        History, theories, concepts, variables
        Empirical studies
        Systematic research synthesis of previous literature
            Narrative reviews
            Meta-analytic reviews
    Interpretation of the Results
        Descriptive presentation of findings: noted relationships, similarities, differences
        Evidence of convergence and divergence of the literature
    Summary and Discussion
        Interpretation of findings: what is known and not known
        Limitations of the review and literature
        Implications and recommendations for social work practice, research, or social policy
References
Tables
Figures
Appendixes

Appendix C

Sample Title Page
for a Journal Manuscript

Risk and   1

Running head: RISK AND PROTECTIVE FACTORS

Risk and Protective Factors

in Child Maltreatment

Barbara Thomlison

Florida International University

Appendix D

Sample Abstract Page

Abstract

This article presents the process and findings
of a study to establish content validity and
reliability in assessing a child's level of
attachment to family. The method employed an
expert panel approach. A 20-person expert panel
was identified to generate a description of the
concept of family reconciliation and a list of
child-family attachment behaviors. A subsequent
150-member expert panel independently rated the
quality of child-family reconciliation of each
child-family attachment behavior on a 7-point
Likert scale ranging from *not very attached*
(1) to *securely attached* (7). Test-retest
reliabilities and coefficient alpha indicated the
process resulted in a valid, reliable, and brief
measure for assessing the level and quality of
child-family reconciliation.

References

American Psychological Association. (2001). *Publication manual of the American Psychological Association* (5th ed.). Washington, DC: Author.

Bem, D. J. (1995). Writing a review article for *Psychological Bulletin. Psychological Bulletin, 118,* 172–177.

Mendelshohn, H. N. (1997). *An author's guide to social work journals* (4th ed.). Washington, DC: NASW Press.

Nicol, A. A. M., & Pexman, P. M. (1999).*Presenting your findings: A practical guide for creating tables.* Washington, DC: American Psychological Association.

Rothery, M. *The "Rules and Regs" page. Thoughts and information on ethics in the Academy.* The URL is *http://fsw.ucalgary.ca/-rothery/ruleregs.html*

Stefani, L., & Carroll, J. (2001). The LTSN Generic Centre Assessment Series No 10. A briefing on plagiarism, Learning and Teaching Support Network. Retrieved August 5, 2002, from *http://www.swap.ac.uk/approaches/Assessment.asp*

Talab, R. S. (2000). Copyright, plagiarism, and Internet-based research projects: Three "golden rules," *Tech Trends, 44* (4), pp. 7–9.

Taylor, S. (1998). *Guidelines for constructing and presenting a poster.* Available through Foster-family Based Treatment Association of North America, 1415 Queen Anne Road, Teaneck, NJ 07666.

Thyer, B. A. (1994). *Successful publishing in scholarly journals.* Thousand Oaks, CA: Sage Publications.

Westerfelt, A., & Dietz, T. J. (1997). *Planning and conducting agency-based research: A workbook for social work students in field placements.* New York: Longman.

Index